Envisioning New Switzerland:

A Founding Document for the Swiss Colonists at Vevay, Indiana

a report by
Ellen Stepleton

Zea Books
Lincoln, Nebraska
2019

Copyright © 2019 Ellen Stepleton.
Revised edition 2020.

ISBN 978-1-60962-149-0
DOI 10.32873/unl.dc.zea.1074

Zea Books are published by the
University of Nebraska–Lincoln Libraries

Cover art: *Kentucky Landscape*, oil on canvas, 1832
by James Pierce Barton, 1817-1891. (public domain)
Original at the Cincinnati Museum Center at Union Terminal

Electronic (pdf) edition available online at
https://digitalcommons.unl.edu/zeabook/

Print edition available from
http://www.lulu.com/spotlight/unllib

UNL does not discriminate based upon any protected status.
Please go to http://www.unl.edu/equity/notice-nondiscrimination

Table of Contents

Acknowledgments ii

Introduction 1

1800 Compact/1800 Lettre 3
    Provenance 3
    Physical description 3
    Document images 5
    Translation 9
    Comments 17

1801 Translation and 1801 Letter 21
    Document images, "1801 Translation" 22
    Transcription of the "1801 Translation" 26
    Document images, "1801 Letter" 29
    Transcription of the "1801 Letter" 31
    Comments 32

Discussion 37

General references 47

Notes 48

Appendix 1. Transcription of 1800 Compact/1800 Lettre 52

Appendix 2. Guide to Dufour-related documents, 1762-1826 58

Acknowledgments

It will surely be evident that this report is the contribution of an amateur rather than an academic historian. My field of endeavor has been geology and vertebrate paleontology, and my livelihood was gained as a fossil preparator. Thus, with this investigation of a historical document, I've necessarily had to function as a compiler rather than a scholar. Any and all value in this report comes from the people I mention here and to these I'm totally indebted. I hope I have adequately reflected their skills and intelligence, and I beg their forgiveness for my own errors and deficiencies.

To Christy Williams I dedicate this project and express my sincere gratitude that she would so generously and patiently provide images of the 1800 Compact/1800 Lettre (in various formats); cheer any progress I made; and ultimately provide for the conservation and preservation of that document.

A meeting with professor Alexandre Dubé, a specialist in the history of the Early Modern Atlantic World at Washington University, was pivotal. During an hour-long interview he decoded the 1800 Compact/1800 Lettre and offered his initial impressions concerning the relative rarity of the document and the context from which it arose.

Thus supplied with some knowledge and fueled by ever-increasing curiosity, I sought to find someone having the patience, interest, and skills necessary to transcribe and translate the Compact. In that cause, Anne Hajek (Modern Language professor at Nebraska Wesleyan University) and Anna Auger Tonkin of Fribourg, Switzerland combined forces with much spirit and good will, and have continued to be delightful colleagues, abettors and critics. It is they who brought the Compact back to life.

Anna and Anne's enthusiasm carried me to the next stage where I could ply archivists and conservators with arcane questions and beg permission to publish document images. These are people who practice in a field similar to my own and whose skills and service I naturally admire and envy, but more to the point, their work preserves the very foundation of history, culture and civilization. Or so I say! For this report Thomas J. McCullough (Moravian Archives, Bethlehem, PA); Laura Eliason (Indiana State Library, Indianapolis, IN); Christine Schmid Engels (Cincinnati History Library and Archives, Cincinnati, OH); and Maggie Callahan (Graphic Conservation Company, Chicago, IL) were remarkably and invaluably helpful.

An observant reader will see that I have cited "Indiana Wine: A History" time and time again. In the absence of that work, I could only have supplied a notice of the 1800 Compact. It is the exhaustive research of James and John Butler that underpins this report, and introduces meaning, context and significance to both the 1800 Compact/1800 Lettre and the 1801 Translation/1801 Letter. I most earnestly recommend their work to anyone interested in the Swiss colonists.

Finally, without the existence of the Switzerland County Historical Society and their unstinting efforts to bring history to the forefront of their community, there would have been no point in writing the report, and thus one less joy in my own life.

INTRODUCTION

This report focusses primarily upon two manuscripts pertaining to the Swiss settlement of Switzerland County, Indiana at the beginning of the 19th century. One manuscript has resided in the collection of the Cincinnati History Library and Archives (CHLA) for over a century and was first cited in a 2001 publication. The other is privately owned and may have entirely escaped the notice of historians. Some of the value of these documents rests in their relation to each other: they are closely linked. Since I am not an academic historian, the best I can do here is call attention to the manuscripts and hope that a more skilled researcher will explore their significance. Scholars with an interest in founding documents, early American communes, early American commercial enterprises, the processes of cultural assimilation, and Swiss-American history are among those for whom these artifacts may have an especial appeal.

But what are they? One (the privately-owned manuscript) is a copy of a compact drafted by a group of would-be immigrants to America. It was signed by them on April 30, 1800 in the valley of Lac de Joux in the canton of Léman (now Vaud), Switzerland. For the purposes of this report, it will be called the "**1800 Compact**." Appended to the compact is a letter dated June 26, 1800 ("**1800 Lettre**") from Daniel Dufour of Montreux, Switzerland to his brother Jean Jaques Dufour of First Vineyard, Kentucky. Jean Jaques Dufour is better known in America as *John James* Dufour, a pioneer of American viticulture. By means of the 1800 Lettre, Daniel was informing Jean Jaques of the immigrants' impending arrival in the United States and of the terms of their agreement, terms to which Jean Jaques would -presumably- also be a party. Indeed, since his arrival in America in 1796, Jean Jaques Dufour had been scouting for both the land and the grapevines that would sustain this band of immigrants and launch an American wine industry. The 1800 Lettre also provides several illuminating details regarding the current state of affairs in Switzerland, both on a familial and a regional level.

The second manuscript dates to mid-February 1801. By then all was in motion. Seventeen immigrants had departed their homes, friends, and relatives in Vaud and were making their way to the French seaport at La Rochelle. Meanwhile in the U.S., after a flurry of letter-writing (to Albert Gallatin, to Thomas Jefferson, and to Congress), Jean Jaques Dufour posted yet another letter on February 11 ("**1801 Letter**") to the Federal Land Office in Cincinnati. With it he enclosed a copy of the 1800 Compact. However *this* copy is an English translation ("**1801 Translation**"), most likely rendered by Jean Jaques Dufour himself. Together, the 1801 Letter and the 1801 Translation comprise the second manuscript, cataloged under the identifier "Mss VF3762" in the collection of the CHLA.

The full story behind these documents is only partly discerned. Even now we have very little information about the circumstances that propelled this group of Swiss artisans and vine-growers towards America. For example, all the surviving children of Jean Jaques Dufour, Sr. would take leave of their father and emigrate to America, including 12-year-old Jean David and 15-year-old Susanne Marguerite. Granted 9-year-old Aimé remained behind, but only temporarily. The elder Dufour owned vineyards and a comfortable residence in Montreux. His family had maintained a relatively high status in their community for generations. Thus, one might have expected that his unmarried daughters and at least one son would remain in Switzerland to conserve their family's social and economic foothold, but no: in this case every bridge was being burnt. The departure of Dufour's two married sons by his first wife, plus three unmarried sons and three unmarried daughters by his second wife, would ultimately and entirely extinguish the family's connection to the Old World. This seems to have been their intention. But why?

Jean Jaques Dufour, Jr. (1763-1827) would later contend that when he first learned of the lamentable absence of wine and vineyards in revolutionary-era America, he at once dedicated his education and his life towards remedying that situation. **(1)** While this may account for *his* actions, it is unlikely that every other sibling and co-immigrant was motivated simply by that purpose. One might argue that the hope of establishing a commercial wine industry in America was a reasonable aspiration for a group of Swiss nationals who shared more compelling reasons for leaving their homeland.

While we know little of the Swiss (departure) side of the equation, the American (arrival and early settlement) side is somewhat better-documented. Many readers of this report will be familiar with the life story of quixotic Jean Jaques Dufour as he tirelessly pursued his elusive goal from 1796 to his death in 1827. Others, through their family histories, may know that while their immigrant forebears made every effort in Indiana to recreate Switzerland's bountiful vineyards and palatable wines, succeeding generations were drawn toward more conventional and rewarding pursuits, agricultural or otherwise. Among several factors, plant pathogens endemic to the New World would forestall the founding of a viable wine industry in the U.S. for many decades. For those unfamiliar with these narratives, the volumes authored by Butler and Butler (2001), John James Dufour (1826, reprinted in 2003), Thomas Pinney (1989), and Julie LeClerc Knox (1942) will be helpful. Of these, James L. and John J. Butler's "Indiana Wine: A History" is most useful for establishing the context of the 1800 Compact, 1801 Translation, and the related letters. In this report I will not be reiterating earlier accounts of the Swiss settlement of Switzerland County, but merely supplying some additional information. In the end, as can be expected, the two manuscripts raise new questions and broaden the arena for future investigations.

1800 Compact and 1800 Lettre

In 2017 while researching Dufour family history, I discovered that a Dufour descendant had posted online images of a 4-page manuscript, handwritten in French, and appearing to be a compact drafted by a group of Vaudois intending to form a colony in America. Moderately acquainted with Switzerland County's early history, I at once recognized several names among the signers of the compact. However, I'd been unaware of any "founding document" in connection to Switzerland County, and thus was very much surprised to see this one. Given that the posted images were small, it was difficult to read the full text, but headings indicated that topics such as education, religious practice, and a communal economy were being addressed. Greatly intrigued, I made inquiries, and the owner of the 1800 Compact/1800 Lettre most graciously and generously provided me with larger scans of the document, and thus began this investigation.

Provenance

Christy Williams, the manuscript's owner, is a descendant of 1801 Swiss immigrants Antoinette *Dufour* Morerod (1781-1857) and Jean Daniel Morerod (1769-1838). Christy's great aunt was Julie LeClerc Knox (1870-1965), author of "The Dufour Saga." While researching that volume, Knox diligently sought old family documents then surviving in Switzerland County households, and some of these were given to her to keep permanently. Perhaps the 1800 Compact/1800 Lettre was one such donation, but if so, it was likely received by Knox <u>after</u> publication of "The Dufour Saga." From Julie Le Clerc Knox the manuscript was inherited by a niece, Louise *Stemmons* Williams, mother of Christy Williams.

In her prologue to "The Dufour Saga," Knox mentioned a "great mass" of Franco-Swiss documents once in the possession of her great uncle, Aimé Jean Rudolf Morerod (1815-1909), Antoinette's only surviving son. It seems that in the mid-19th century the residence of Antoinette *Dufour* Morerod became a repository for certain Dufour artifacts, in part because Antoinette outlived most of her siblings, but also because the Morerod home was very much a cultural center for the Swiss emigres. It's therefore conceivable that a document originally belonging to Jean Jaques Dufour but having significance for the entire community found its way to either Antoinette or her son. However, one cannot state definitively that this was the case.

Physical Description

Two 9 ³⁄₈" x 15 ¹⁄₈" leaves containing four full pages of text have survived as an incomplete document. The 1800 Compact occupies the first three and two-thirds pages. Immediately following the signatures to that agreement, the 1800 Lettre commences with the heading "A Sales de Montreux___ Du 26 Juin 1800." The remaining third of page 3 and all of page 4 are the 1800 Lettre. Page 4 ends in mid-sentence with the words "...a passé en revue trois" with "demi" below, indicating the word "demi" will begin page 5. Alas, page 5 (the next leaf) is missing. Not only are we denied the writer's description of some stirring events, but also his closing signature, the panel for Jean Jaques Dufour's address, remnants of the seal, and any postal markings. Thankfully, internal evidence ("...I've signed the document in that hope," e.g.) establishes that the writer <u>was</u> Daniel Dufour (age 35) writing to his full brother Jean Jaques Dufour (age 37). Daniel not only signed the 1800 Compact for the Dufour family as its nominal head, but was also acting as a leader or co-leader of the colonists at this time.

In 2017, the condition of the 1800 Compact and 1800 Lettre was delicate. Through age and wear, the short-fibered paper had become soft, very fragile, and cockled. Certain areas of text were totally or partially obscured along creases, at folded corners, and along frayed and folded margins. An area of paper loss occurred near the top of the first leaf, and also in that leaf's mid-section crease. The second leaf was even more severely damaged at mid-section. Fortunately, the contrast between ink and paper was marked, and the surviving script in most places was readily discerned.

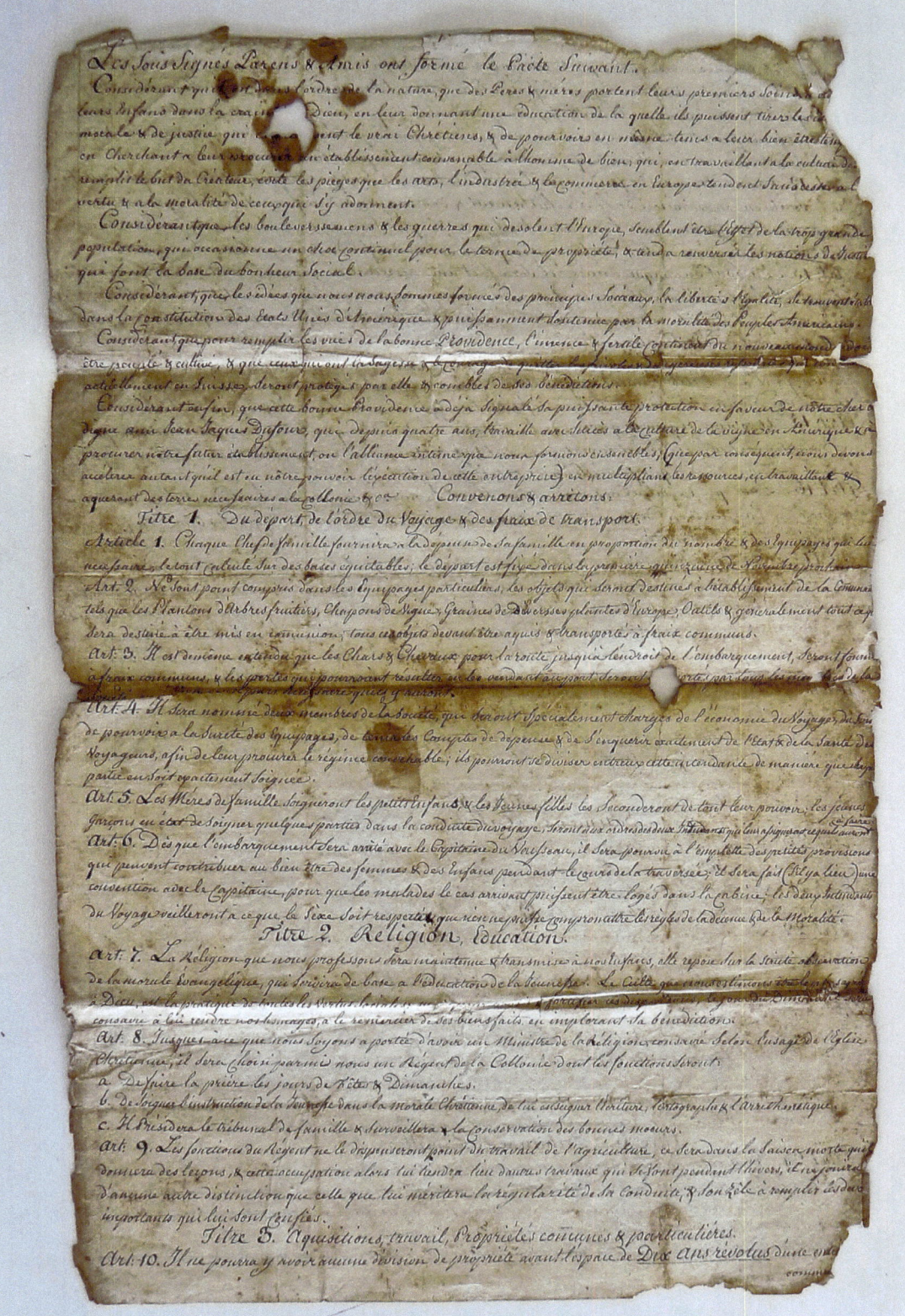

Fig. 1. page 1, 1800 Compact before restoration

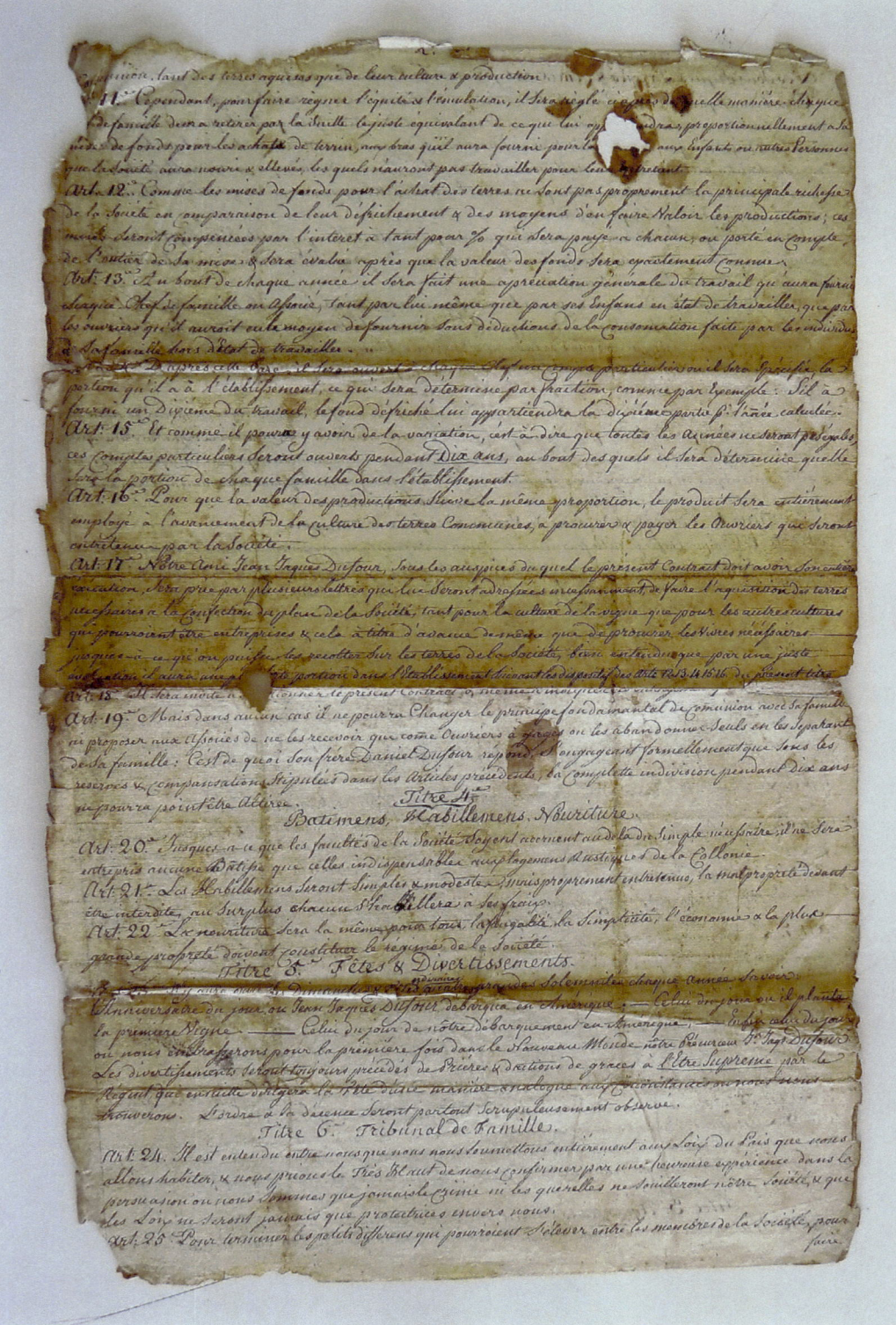

Fig. 2. page 2, 1800 Compact before restoration

Fig. 3. page 3, showing the closure of the 1800 Compact and the beginning of the 1800 Lettre, before restoration.

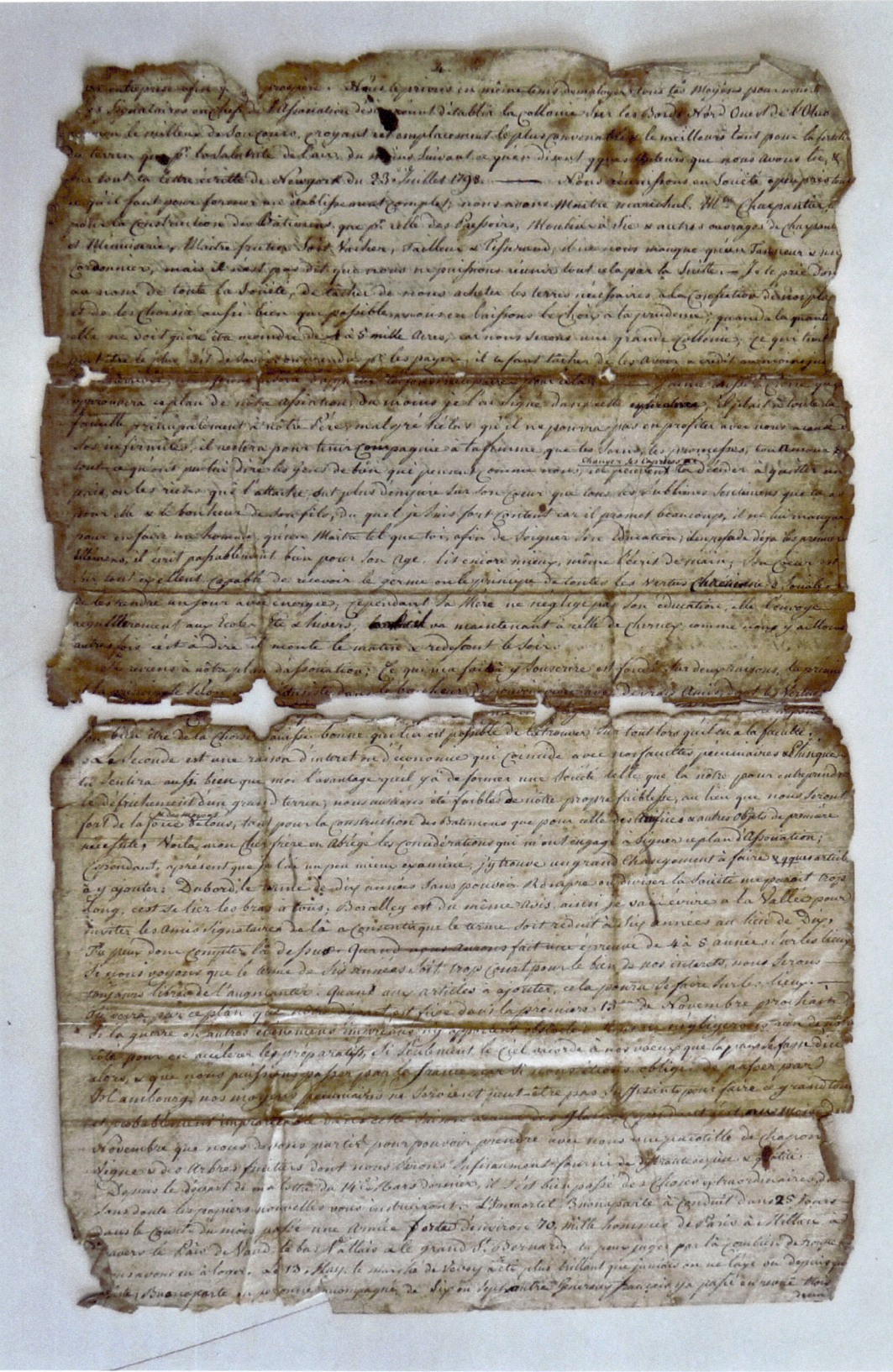

Fig. 4. page 4, 1800 Lettre before restoration

Transcription of "1800 Compact/1800 Lettre"

In 2018, two individuals (Anne Hajek and Anna Auger Tonkin) prepared separate transcriptions and translations of the 1800 Compact/1800 Lettre, using 11" x 17" photocopies of digital scans. The manuscript had not yet received the attention of a paper conservator, and not every word or phrase was retrievable from the original, let alone from photocopies.

The two transcriptions were almost identical, although formatted differently. For this report, a line by line rendition is supplied in Appendix 1.

Translation of "1800 Compact/1800 Lettre"

The following translation of the 1800 Compact/1800 Lettre was developed by Anne Hajek and Anna Auger Tonkin. Bold font, indents and paragraph spacing have been introduced to enhance legibility. Bracketed ellipses [... ...] mark areas of missing or illegible text. Words within brackets are inferences or, if italicized, editorial insertions.

The undersigned relatives and friends have formed the following pact:

Considering that it is in the natural order that fathers and mothers take greatest care to raise their children in [the fear] of God, giving them an education from which they can draw [the concepts] of morality and justice that characterize true Christians, while at the same time providing for their [temporal] well-being, by seeking to procure for them a condition worthy of a virtuous person who, by working to cultivate [the earth,] fulfills the goal of the Creator and avoids the traps that art, industry, and commerce in Europe set ceaselessly to spoil [the] virtue and morality of those who indulge in them.

Considering that the upheavals and wars that afflict Europe seem to be the result of its over-population, which causes persistent disruption of property ownership and tends to undermine the notions that form the basis of societal happiness.

Considering that our ideas on social principles, liberty, and equality are established in the Constitution of the United States of America and are powerfully supported by the morality of the American people.

Considering that, in order to fulfill the will of Providence, the immense and fertile New World will be populated and cultivated, and those with the wisdom and courage to leave the currently frivolous and dangerous state of affairs in Switzerland will be protected and blessed by heaven.

Considering, finally, that this divine Providence has already shown its powerful protection of our dear and worthy friend Jean Jaques Dufour who, for four years, has been working successfully to grow grapes in America and to procure our future settlement *[for]* the intimate alliance that we are forming together (as a result, we must hasten as much as we can the execution of this enterprise) by developing resources, and by working & acquiring the lands necessary for our Colony, etc.

Let us agree and put in writing:

Title 1. Departure, Organization of Voyage, and Transportation Costs

Article 1:   Each head of household will provide for the expenses of his family in proportion to the number of individuals and the supplies necessary to support them, the whole sum calculated on an equitable basis. The departure is set for the first two weeks of next November.

Article 2:   Supplies destined for the establishment of the Community will not be considered part of the individual family expenses. These include cuttings for fruit trees, grapevine shoots, seeds for diverse European plants, tools, & generally anything that will be used communally; all these items will be acquired and transported at shared expense.

Article 3.   It is likewise understood that the costs of wagons and horses necessary for travel to the point of boarding, and any losses that might result from selling them at the port, will be shared by all the members of our society.

Article 4.   Two members of the society will be nominated to deal specifically with the expenses of the voyage, to support and provide for the safety of the equipages, to handle the expense accounts, and to inquire as to the state of health of the travelers, in order to procure for them a suitable diet; they can divide between them this administrative work so that each part of it is managed properly.

Article 5:   The mothers will care for the small children, and the young girls will help them to the best of their ability; the young boys capable of assisting in the management of the voyage will be directed by *[the]* two overseers who will assign them their tasks.

Article 6:   Once boarding has been initiated by the ship's captain, we will see to the purchase of some small provisions that might contribute to the wellbeing of the women and children during the voyage. If possible, an agreement will be made with the captain that the sick, should the case arise, be lodged in the cabin; the two overseers will ensure that the women are respected and that nothing compromises the rules of decency and morality.

Title 2: Religion, Education

Article 7:   The religion that we profess will be upheld and passed on to our children; it relies on strict adherence to the morals of the Gospel, which will serve as the basis for the education of our youth. The faith that we esteem to be the most agreeable to God is the practice of all the social virtues, but to nourish and strengthen this disposition, Sunday will be consecrated to His worship *[and to]* expressing gratitude for his gifts through beseeching his blessing.

Article 8: Until we have an official Minister of Religion, consecrated according to the custom of the Christian church, we will choose from among us a Regent to serve the Colony as follows:
    a. To lead prayers on Sundays and feast days
    b. To oversee the instruction of youth in Christian Morality and to teach them writing, spelling, and arithmetic.
    c. To preside over the Family Tribunal and to ensure the conservation of good morals.

Article 9. The functions of the Regent will not exempt him from agricultural work; he will only teach lessons in the off season, and thus this occupation will take the place of other work that is done during winter, but he will not enjoy any distinction other than that which is earned through his good conduct and his zeal to fulfill the important duties conferred upon him.

Title 3: Acquisitions, Work, Common and Privately Held Property

Article 10: There can be no division of communal property (including the land and its proceeds) until ten years have passed.

[Article 11]: To ensure that equity and emulation reign, the manner by which each head of family will be able to withdraw afterwards the just equivalent of what belongs to him will be proportionate to the capital which he gave for the purchase of land, the labor that he will have provided for the [... ...]
to the children or other persons that the society feeds and raises, who do not work to provide for themselves.

Article 12: The funds initially contributed by each family towards the purchase of communal property are not in and of themselves the principal wealth of the Colony. Rather, lands cleared and made capable of agricultural production will be of even greater value. All of these inputs will be factored in a percentage interest that will be paid to each family, to be established after the value of the whole is known exactly.

Article 13: At the end of each year, a general assessment will be made of the work that each family has done, that is, the work done by the head of the family, his children (those in a condition to work), as well as by any workers that he might have been able to hire, minus the consumption of the individuals in the family not in a condition to work.

Article 14: From this assessment, each head of household will have access to an individual account containing funds reserved for his share of the venture, which will be determined by fraction. For example, if he furnishes one-tenth of the work, the reserved funds that will belong to him will be one-tenth for the calculated year.

Article 15: As there might be variance, which is to say that every year will not be the same, these individual accounts will be open for ten years; at the end of this term, the portion for each family will be determined.

Article 16: So that the value of their production will follow the same proportion, proceeds will be spent entirely on improving the cultivation of common fields and procuring and paying for workers hired and supported at the expense of the society.

Article 17: Our friend Jean Jaques Dufour, under whose the auspices the present contract must be implemented, will be asked in several letters, addressed to him in the near future, to purchase the properties necessary to carry out the plans of the Society for the cultivation of vines as well as alternative crops that might be introduced, and, by way of advance financing, to procure the supplies necessary for our survival until the first harvest on our lands. It is understood that the sum will be evaluated justly so that he receives his fair share of the settlement, following the devices of Articles 12, 13, 14, 15, 16 of the present title.

Article 18: He will be invited by mail to review the present contract and even to indicate any changes that suit him.

Article 19: But in no case will he, with his family, be permitted to change the fundamental principle of Communion nor to propose that the Associates be treated only as workers, or to abandon them *[the Associates]* by separating them from his family: that is what his brother Daniel guarantees, formally acknowledging that according to the stipulations of the preceding articles, that the complete communion of the Society for a period of ten years cannot in any way be changed.

Title 4: Buildings, Clothing, Food

Article 20: Until the Society has accumulated more resources than those which are strictly necessary, they will not attempt to build more than essential, rustic lodgings for the Colony.

Article 21: Clothing shall be simple and modest, but clean and well-maintained; uncleanliness being forbidden; moreover, each person will be clothed at their own expense.

Article 22: The diet of the Society shall be the same for all and shall be characterized by frugality, simplicity, economy, and the greatest hygiene.

Title 5: Celebrations and Amusements

Article 23: Other than Sundays and the usual holidays, there shall be four great celebrations each year. They are: the anniversary of the day when Jean Jaques

Dufour left for America; the anniversary of the day when he planted the first vine; the anniversary of our departure for America; and finally, the anniversary of the day when we will embrace our precursor Jean Jaques Dufour for the first time in the New World.

The festivities will always be preceded by prayers and thanksgivings to the Supreme Being by the Regent, who will then direct the celebration in a manner fitting with our circumstances. Order and decency in every situation will be scrupulously observed.

Title 6: Family Tribunal

Article 24:   It is understood among us that we submit ourselves entirely to the laws of the country that we will inhabit, and we pray to the Most High to fulfill our belief that crime and quarrels will never even be named among our Society, and that the laws of that country will never be anything but protective of us.

Article 25:   To end any small differences that might arise among the members of the Society, in order to ensure that decency is respected and to maintain the strict morality of members as well as to discourage laziness and negligence, there will be a Family Tribunal made up of the four oldest members of the Society and presided over by the Regent. Additionally the Accused will have the right to choose, if he feels inclined to do so, two other members of the Society, thereby increasing the number of judges by two members.

Article 26:   The Family Tribunal will pronounce judgments on all the cases mentioned in the preceding articles. It can inflict penalties and humiliations, such as assigning the guilty party to a certain type of work; a separate eating place, and inferior food compared to that of the normal meals; the deprivation of diversions for a limited time; and even monetary fines that will be placed in the family accounts and set aside for the purchase of paper, pens, and books useful to the youth.

Article 27:   On the contrary, those who distinguish themselves through their love of work, activity, industriousness, and above all by exemplary conduct, will receive encouragement and marks of good will on behalf of the Society, such as a seat at the head of the table, a place of distinction during festivities, a crown of honor, bouquets of flowers on Sunday; moreover, they shall receive the gift of clothes to wear on feast days.

Title 7: Unforseen Events

Article 28:   It is agreed that in the case of the death of a head of family or his representative, be it during the voyage or in the Colony, the widow and orphans will not be in any way deprived of any of the advantages of the Society, which will adopt them and, in all things, represent the interests of the deceased individual, receiving and admitting them in all respects in his place.

Article 29:   It is possible that once we are present on the lands of the projected establishment, it could be appropriate to make some changes to the present conditions, to add new articles, which can be proposed by a member of the Society, as long as two thirds plus one give their consent, but in no case can we discuss making changes to the principle of communion for ten years, nor to override in any way article 28.

Article 30:   The thirds mentioned in the previous article will be counted as follows: the third of five will be two, the third of eight will be three, the third of eleven will be four, and so on; this calculation will be made anytime that the number of voters cannot be equally divided into thirds.

Article 31:   Every time that there are changes to be made that require deliberation on proposals, the outcome will be decided by a general council made up of the heads of family or constructed so as to include the mothers of each family and young men having reached the age of twenty. They [... ...]

The thiry-one articles of this contract will be upheld religiously by all parties. [... ...] we give as our guarantee our free and sincere affirmation in the name of the Supreme Being, whose blessings we implore and to whom we commit our present and future possessions.

Duly completed and signed in Chenit, district of the Vallée du Lac de Joux, Canton Léman in Switzerland, the thirtieth of April, one thousand eight hundred___30th April 1800.

The original signed by

Daniel Dufour of Montreux
David Golay of Vallée du Lac de Joux
Philippe Berney "   "
Joseph Meylan   "   "
Jean Pierre Daniel Borralley of Blonay, Master Carpenter

(all in the name of their respective families)

at Sales de Montreux—26 June 1800.
My beloved brother and dear friend! The 14th of last March, I gave a letter for you to citizen Genand of Vevey, the son of Tourneur, and his friend Trottet (son of the one who has the baths behind Aile), who left the next day for Bordeaux, planning to embark from there to America, but I have just learned from their fathers that they did not embark, because they found the weather too dangerous, and

especially because the price of boarding was too expensive; so, they went on into Spain, putting off the journey until the circumstances are more favorable, and I don't actually know if they sent my letter or not; because of my uncertainty, I will repeat some of the same information in this letter.

I received your delightful letter from Firstvineyard near Lexington in Kentucky, dated the October 15, 1799, plus a short letter included in one from Mr. Mennet to his father in Lausanne, same date; in the first I see that you were rejoicing, as was the whole family, to be able to embrace one another this spring; but alas, our hopes were disappointed yet again; nevertheless, things are getting better, political events appear to be taking a favorable turn, day by day, toward peace, and I hope that over the course of January or February 1801, the family (accompanied by the friends who will, God willing, found the colony outlined in the pact preceding this letter) will have the sweet pleasure of embracing you. Oh, my dear brother! May this hope fill our hearts with joy; all our wishes are addressed to the Supreme Being that He might, in his infinite mercy, bless our enterprise so it might prosper. We pray, at the same time, that He will help you to do all that you can for us.

The signatories or members of the Association desire to establish the colony on the northwest banks of the Ohio *[the Northwest Territory-ed.]* at the middle of its course, believing this placement the most conducive and the best in terms of both the fertility of the soil and the salubrity of the air; at least according to what some authors say whom we have read on the subject, and especially based on your letter written in New York the 23rd of July 1798.

In the Society, we have assembled just about everything that we will need to form a complete settlement; we have a master blacksmith, a master carpenter for the construction of the buildings as well as presses, saw mills and other works of carpentry and woodwork, a master orchardist, a cattleman, a tailor and a weaver; we are only missing a tanner and a shoemaker, but it goes without saying that we could figure all that out later.

So, I plead with you, in the name of the whole society, to try to buy the necessary lands for the fulfillment of our plans, and to choose them as well as possible; we give the decision to your care; as for the quantity, it must be at least four to five thousand acres, because we will be a large colony; what will probably be most difficult for you is knowing where to borrow in order to buy the lands; you must try to get them by credit, at least until our arrival, as we will bring the necessary funds for their purchase.

I would like to think that you will approve our plan of association; at least, I've signed it in that hope. It was pleasing to the whole family, especially our father, in spite of the fact that he will not experience it with us due to his infirmities. He will remain in the company of your wife who cannot be convinced (despite your cares, your promises, your love, and all that good people who think like us have told her) to leave a country where little things have more sway over her heart than the sublime sentiments you have for her and for the happiness of her son, with whom I am very content because he is very promising.

To become a man he is lacking only a teacher such as yourself to care for his education. He already possesses the beginning elements: he writes passably well for his age, reads even better, even handwriting; above all, his heart is excellent, capable of receiving the seed or the principles of all the Christian and societal virtues, and to fulfill them one day with energy. However, his mother does not neglect his education. She sends him regularly to both the winter and summer schools. He now attends the one in Chernex, as we used to long ago, that is to say, he goes up in the morning and returns in the evening.

Returning to our plan of association; my acceptance thereof is founded upon two reasons. The first principle being the happiness of living with true friends whose virtues [... ...] or wellbeing to choose it to the best of his ability, to find it as soon as he is able. The second is a reason of economy that coincides with our monetary abilities, something that you understand as well as I; that is, the advantage that there is in forming a society such as ours to undertake the clearing of a large amount of land; we would have been weakened by our own flaws, whereas we will be strong with the strength and abilities of us all, through the construction of buildings and devices and other necessities.

There you have it, my dear brother: the considerations, in brief, that have led me to sign this plan of association. However, now that I have better examined it, I find there is a large change to be made and some articles to add. First, the term of ten years without dividing the Society's properties seems too long to me; our hands would all be tied. Boralley is of the same opinion, so I am going write to La Vallée to invite our friends who have signed to consent that the term be reduced to six years instead of ten. You can count on it. After a period of four to five years on site, if we see that a six-year term is too short for our best interests, we will still be free to increase it. As for the articles to add, that also can be done on site.

You will see by this plan that our departure is set for the first fortnight of next November, provided war or other unforeseen events don't hinder us; we will not neglect anything on our end to hasten the preparations. If only Heaven would grant our wish for peace here, we could travel through France; for if we are obliged to go through Hamburg, our funds might be insufficient for the entirety of the trip, and it would probably be infeasible because that's the icy season; regardless, we must depart in November in order to take with us an assemblage of vine and fruit tree cuttings that will ensure we have sufficient varieties and quantities of quality plants.

Since sending my letter last March 14, many extraordinary things have transpired, of which the newspapers have doubtless informed you. The Immortal Bonaparte, in 25 days last month, brought about 70,000 men from Paris to Milan across Vaud, the lower Valais, and the Grand-Saint-Bernard; you can judge for yourself how many troops we had to lodge. May 13, the Vevey market was more active than we had seen since [... ...] Bonaparte himself came through, accompanied by six or seven other French generals three

half-

Comments

1. Note that the signers of this, the 30 Avril 1800 Compact, were Daniel Dufour (on behalf of his wife and six siblings); David Golay (representing his wife and at least ten children); Philippe Berney (and family?); Joseph Meylan (and family?); and Jean Pierre Daniel Boralley (having a wife and two children).

Of these, the Berneys and Meylans did not, in the end, undertake the journey, and the Golay family was much delayed. This appears to have been a major setback for the colony: perhaps Berney and Meylan represented large families with substantial financial assets, now greatly missed. Dufour's February 1, 1801 letter to Thomas Jefferson had referred to "four great respectable families" joining with the Dufours to form the colony. **(2)** But in his January 15, 1802 letter to Jefferson, although he can report the arrival of "five families of wine growers" and his expectation that others will soon follow, Dufour is forced to admit that the five families "are all poor people who had merely enough for their travel." He goes on to state "...Our petition is the same as last year except for the amount; I was requesting at that time a large tract [7,000 acres] because a large Colony had formed ... but because of the war this association was broken and only a small part of the company came." **(3)** A few days earlier Daniel Dufour had written to Albert Gallatin, then the U.S. Treasury Secretary, noting that only 2000 acres were required by the settlers. "We do not wish to extend the bounds of honesty. My brother in requesting 7000 acres was counting on the arrival of numerous colonists, but several members of the colony could not follow us because of last minute inconveniences, caused by our revolution." **(4)** A reduction of 5,000 acres signals a considerable decline in the colony's ambitions, prospects, and wherewithal.

Despite the defections and disruptions, two new families had joined with the Dufours and Boralleys by March 1801. These were the Siebentahls (François Louis and his son, Jean François) and Bettens (Jean François Philippe Bettens, his wife Jeanne Rose Judith and daughter Jeanne Marie Charlotte). Also, a solitary young man named Jean Daniel Morerod had suddenly been inspired to try his luck in America, and thus he too was counted among the seventeen Swiss passengers boarding the *Voodsop*, lying off La Rochelle, on March 20.

In the end, Congress would allocate 2520 acres for the purposes of the Swiss colonists with payment due in 1814, and full forgiveness of interest. **(5,6)** Over the next several years Jean Jaques Dufour contributed about 1111 more acres to the original tract, purchasing these at the standard rate. **(7,8)** Accordingly New Switzerland swelled to about 3631 acres. Even more encouraging must have been the steady arrival of additional families from Switzerland. A surname index on the genealogical website "The Swiss Settlement of Switzerland County, Indiana," compiled by John W. McCoy, gives a startling indication of how the initial settlement of five families may have encouraged many others to migrate. **(9)**

2. The 1800 Compact owned by Christy Williams is not the original document bearing the actual signatures of Dufour, Berney, et. al. Where *that* document may be, or what fate befell it, is unknown. Secondly, it is quite possible that *several* copies of the compact were made in 1800. For instance, it is highly likely that Daniel Dufour would have sent a duplicate of the 1800

Compact/1800 Lettre to his brother Jean Jaques. Given the risks and vagaries posed by maritime navigation, ill-organized postal services, warfare, and spies (French, British, and Swiss), not to mention the ordinary mishaps and changes of plan that any person entrusted with a letter was apt to encounter or create, it seems highly likely that Daniel would have tried to communicate to Jean Jaques through several avenues. We know that this was the practice of Jean Jaques Dufour when writing to his family in Switzerland, at least on some occasions, **(10)** so the reverse would seem also to apply: especially in a matter as important and time-sensitive as this.

3. The letter attached to the compact is, for now, the only known surviving letter from Switzerland concerning the arrangements, the thoughts, and circumstances of the soon-to-be immigrants. We learn for instance that Jean Jaques Dufour, Sr. is ailing and unable to contemplate a move to America. Likewise Jean Jaques Dufour, Jr.'s wife is quite unwilling to come, although it has been over four years since she has seen her husband. While Daniel's reference to "the Immortal Bonaparte" most likely signals the Dufour family's whole-hearted support of the First Consul, no doubt the passage of 70,000 troops through Vaud had left its mark on their orchards, pastures, and thoroughfares.

Light is shed, also, on the matter of site selection. By this time the colonists knew that Jean Jaques Dufour was based in Kentucky and developing a vineyard owned by shareholders, the "Kentucky Vineyard Society." The colonists might have chosen to place their vineyards nearby along the Kentucky River, but Daniel Dufour makes the colonists' wishes explicitly clear: they intend to locate in the Northwest Territory. The purported "salubrity of the air" and fertile soils of that country appear to be influencing their decision. Other factors may or may not have entered into their thinking. The cost and availability of land, topography (with southern exposures being most favorable for vineyards), concerns about Dufour's association with the Lexington investors, and slavery- all of these come to mind.

4. Assuming that Daniel Dufour dispatched his letter on about June 27, 1800 and that no extraordinary delays were encountered in transit, then Jean Jaques Dufour may have received it as early as September 1800. Notably, on August 5, 1800 Jean Jaques Dufour had entered into a contractual relationship with the shareholders of the Kentucky Vineyard Society under which he would be obliged to plant and manage their vineyard ("First Vineyard") in Jessamine County, Kentucky for nine years. **(11)** This arrangement complicated his relationship with the Swiss colonists but in some ways would prove beneficial to all concerned.

Fig. 5. The harbor at La Rochelle as it appeared in 1762. It was here that the sloop *Useful*, on March 20, 1801 took aboard the Swiss immigrants and their cargo. She ferried them out 3 miles where the "superb ship *Voodsop*" lay anchored. After a spate of foul weather and another trip back to La Rochelle for more provisions, the Swiss were finally underway on March 25. Within several hours *Voodsop* was intercepted first by a British frigate, then a Guernsey corsair, and lastly by a 74-gun British man-of-war. **(12)** Identity papers and other corroborating documents were essential if these francophone Swiss could entertain any hope of reaching the U.S. unmolested. Possibly a copy of the 1800 Compact was proffered to help establish their bona fides with the English captains. ["Vue du Port de La Rochelle." 1762. Oil on canvas. Artist: Claude-Joseph Vernet. Musée national de la Marine, La Rochelle, France. public domain.]

1801 Translation and 1801 Letter

Once acquainted with the 1800 Compact, I found it difficult to believe that it had eluded the attention of Switzerland County's earliest documentarians. Therefore, I carefully re-read Perret Dufour's "Swiss Settlement of Switzerland County, Indiana," Weakley, Harraman & Co.'s "History of Dearborn, Ohio, and Switzerland Counties, Indiana," and Knox's "The Dufour Saga" as well as several shorter 19th century accounts. Indeed none of these mentioned a founding document.

Belatedly, through an internet search combining "John James Dufour" with various other search terms I encountered a reference to "Indiana Wine: A History." Only then did I realize that a more recent historical account of the Swiss colony even existed. Quick to obtain a copy, I rejoiced to see that this was a comprehensive and scholarly study, meticulously researched and containing a wealth of new information. In fact, "Indiana Wine" is the indispensable starting point for any investigation into the life of Jean Jaques Dufour and the accomplishments garnered by the Swiss colony. And it is here, finally and justly, that the Compact makes its first appearance in the historical record, if I am not mistaken. If I was momentarily crestfallen to discover that the 1800 Compact was not entirely unknown, my disappointment was more than compensated by the invaluable information gained from "Indiana Wine."

Its authors quoted several passages from the compact, noting that their source was an original document in the collection of the CHLA. I might not have pursued the matter further except for the fact that a letter was said to accompany this version of the Compact. It had been written by Jean Jaques Dufour; was addressed to the Federal Land Office in Cincinnati, Ohio; and dated from February 11, 1801. I was sufficiently curious to want to read the letter. The CHLA kindly provided scans of both the compact and the letter, and here again I was to be surprised. Their's was *not* a copy of the 1800 Compact after all, but instead an English translation of it.

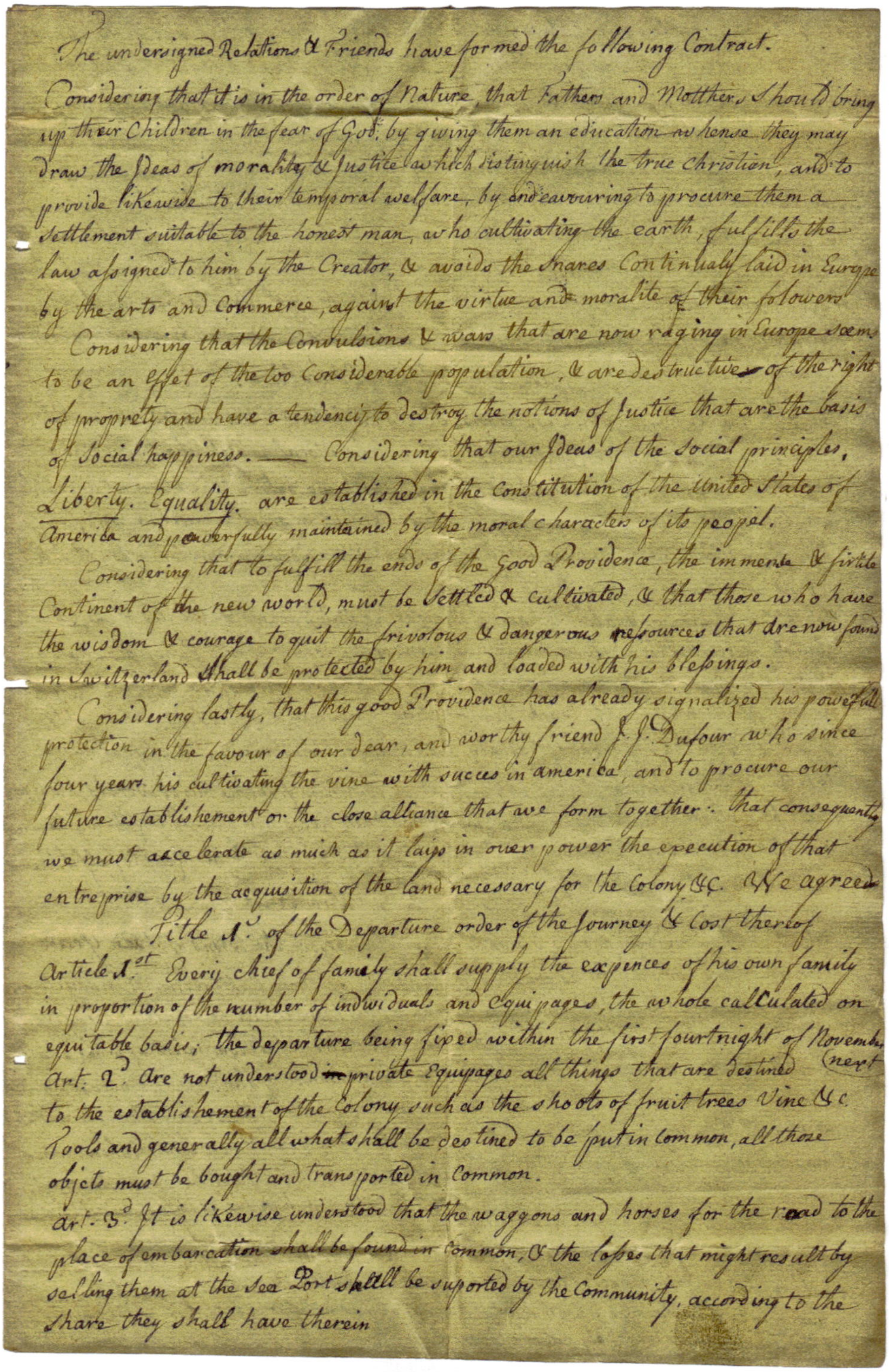

Document Images, 1801 Translation

The undersigned Relations & Friends have formed the following Contract.

Considering that it is in the order of Nature, that Fathers and Mothers should bring up their Children in the fear of God, by giving them an education whence they may draw the Ideas of morality & Justice which distinguish the true Christian, and to provide likewise to their temporal welfare, by endeavouring to procure them a Settlement suitable to the honest man, who cultivating the earth, fulfills the law assigned to him by the Creator, & avoids the Snares Continually laid in Europe by the arts and Commerce, against the virtue and moralite of their folowers.

Considering that the Convulsions & wars that are now raging in Europe seem to be an effect of the too Considerable population, & are destructive of the right of proprety and have a tendency to destroy the notions of Justice that are the basis of Social happiness. — Considering that our Ideas of the Social principles, Liberty, Equality, are established in the Constitution of the United States of America and powerfully maintained by the moral characters of its peopel.

Considering that to fulfill the ends of the good Providence, the immense & fertile Continent of the new world, must be Settled & cultivated, & that those who have the wisdom & courage to quit the frivolous & dangerous resources that are now found in Switzerland shall be protected by him and loaded with his blessings.

Considering lastly, that this good Providence has already signalized his powerfull protection in the favour of our dear, and worthy friend J.J. Dufour who since four years his cultivating the vine with succes in america, and to procure our future establishement or the close alliance that we form together: that consequently we must accelerate as much as it lays in our power the execution of that entreprise by the acquisition of the land necessary for the Colony &c. We agreed

Title 1.ˢ of the Departure order of the Journey & Cost therof

Article 1.ˢᵗ Every chief of family shall supply the expences of his own family in proportion of the number of indwiduals and equipages, the whole calculated on equitable basis; the departure being fixed within the first fourtnight of November next

Art. 2.ᵈ Are not understood in private equipages all things that are destined to the establishement of the Colony such as the shoots of fruit trees Vine &c. Tools and generally all what shall be destined to be put in common, all those objects must be bought and transported in common.

Art. 3.ᵈ It is likewise understood that the waggons and horses for the road to the place of embarcation shall be found in common, & the losses that might result by selling them at the sea Port shall be suported by the Community, according to the share they shall have therein

Fig. 6. Page 1, 1801 Translation, Mss VF3763
(courtesy of Cincinnati History Library and Archive)

Art. 4th There shall be nominated two members of the society that shall be specially charged with the Œconomy of the voyage, of the Care and safety of the equipages, to keep the book of account to enquire exactly into the care and health of the travellers so as to procure them convenient diet, they may divide among themselves this stewarship so that every thing is carefully attended to

Art. 5th The mothers of family shall take care of the little children, & the young girls will second them with all their power. The Boys able to do any things shall be at the orders of the two stewards

Art. 6: As soon as the embarcation shall be arrested with the Capt. of the ships there shall be provided as many small provisions as may contribute to the ease of the Women & Children at sea; there shall be made if necessary an agreem.t with the Capt. so as to loge the sicks as conveniently as possible. the two stewards shall be carefull that the sex shall be respected & order & decency exactly observed.

Title 2.º Religion Education

Art. 7th The Religion which we profess shall be maintained & transmitted to our children it rests upon the strict observation of the Evangelic Moral which shall serve as a Basis to the education of youth, the Worship which we belive to be the most agreable to God, is the practice of all the Social virtues, but in order to ascertain and fortify those dispositions every Sunday shall be consecrated to render him our homages, thank him for his benefit and implore his blessings.

Art. 8th Till we are enabled to have a Minister apointed according the use of the Christian Church there shall be chose among us a Regent of the Colony whose functions shall be 1º to say priers on Sundays and holly days. 2º to take Care of the instruction of Y[outh] in the Christian morality, teach them Writing. Grammar Cyphering &c. 3º to Preside the Tribunal of Family and to inspect the preservation of good moral

Art. 9th The functions of the Regent shall not prevent him from his rural works, his leçons shall be given only in the dead season, when they shall keep him the place of the winter work; he shall enjoy no other distinction but that to which his virtues & his zeal to fulfil the duties of his station will entitle him to.

Title 3 Properties

Art. 10th There can not be no division of properties before the terms of ten Years from an entire Communion as well of the lands as of their Cultivation & productions.

Art 11 however, to maintain equity & emulation there shall be regulated hereafter in what manner ever chief of family shall afterwards retire a just equivalent of what shall belong to him in proportion of his first funds for the acquisition of lands, the number of hands he had found for the culture, Children & other persons suported by the society whom are unable to work

Art 12º As the purchase money is not considered by the Society as its principal richess, when compared to the clearing and Culture, the purchase money shall be compensated by bearing interest which shall be paid to every one or give credit in his account and shall be after it has been fixed when the value of said funds shall be know exactly.

Art 13 At the end of every year there shall be made a général evaluation of the work that shall be found by Every Chief of family or his partner as well by himself as by his children able to work or by the workmen he should have the means of finding after a deduction of the consomption of the individuals of his family not able to work

Art. 14 After this principle there shall be kept to each Chief a open account where shall be specified what share he has in the settlement, by giving credit to him at the end of each year for the work he has done.

Art. 15. And as there may be some variation & all the years may not be equal, those private account shall be kept open during ten years, at the end of which shall be determined what share each family

Art. 16. That the productions of the farm follow the same proportion, they shall be entirely employ to the emprouvement of the land, by paying the wages of hire hands, buildings &C.

Art. 17 Our friend J.J. Dufour under whose auspices the present contract is to have its entire execution shall be invited by several Letters to make the acquisition of the Lands that are necessary to the plan of the society as well for the Culture of the vine as to any other sort of Culture that may be carried on by the Society, and the provisions for the sustainement of the colony till they may be obtain from our own Cultivation.

Art. 18. He shall be invited to sanction the present contract & even indicate the changements he will think proper

Art. 19. But in no instance shall he be able to alter the fundamental principle of Comunity neither propose to any of the present Members to receive him as workman under wages or forsake him alone by separating him from his family: His brother D.n Dufour binds himself formelly into the execution of this present article, & that under the reserve & compensation stipulated by the precedents articles the Complete indivision of ten years can not be altered.

Title 4. Buildings Dress & Diet

Art. 20. Untill the faculties of the Society be increased beyond the bare necessaires of life, no buildings shall be undertaken but what shall be deemed indispensably necessary to the rural logings of the Colony

Art. 21. The Dress shall be plain & modest, but cleanly kept uncleanliness being forbid each one owever shall find his own clothes,

Art. 22. The Diet shall be the same for all, frugality, planiness, economy and the greatest cleanliness must constitute the regiment of the Society.

Title 5. Feast and Diversions

Art. 23. Beside Sunday and Holidays there shall be 4 great feastivals in the year to be fixed afterward, which shall be the anniversary of the four greatest events arrived for the best of the Society, allthough the anniversary of the planting of the first vineyard shall be one of them; the Diversions shall always be preceded by thanksgiving to the Almighty by the Regent who afterwards shall order the diversions in a manner suitable to our Circumstances — order and decency shall be regularly observed.

Title 6. Tribunal of Family

Art. 24. It is to be understood that we submit ourselves entirely to the laws of the Country we are going to inhabit & we beg the Almighty to comfirm us by an happy experience in the persuasion we are that never either Crime nor quarrel will soil our Society and that the laws shall only serve us as protectors

Art. 25. In order to terminate all the litle difference that might arrise between the members of the Society, to maintain decency as well as a Strict morality, likewise to repress idleness & neglects there shall be a Tribunal of family Composed of four of the Eldest of the Society and presided by the Regent, besides two other members of the Society which the Defendant

Defendant will have a right to chose, and by these means augment of two the number of his Juges
Art. 26. The tribunal of family shall pronounce arbitrarily upon all the cases mentioned in the precedent article, he may inflict Pains & chastiments, such as to asign to the culprit a separat place & different victuals from the rest, the privation of the diversions for a limited time, and even pecuniary fines, which shall be destined to buy some Books useful to the youth.
Art. 27. Those on the contrary who shall be distinguished by their love of work, their industry & activity, and examplary behaviour, shall receive encouragement from the Society such as the first seat at table, places of honour in the Diversions, crowns of honnour, Nosegays on Sundays besides a present of some dress for their wearing on Sundays.

Title 7. Unforeseen Events

Art. 28. It is agreed that in case of Death, either in the Journey or in the colony of a chief of family or his representant, the widow and orphans shall not be deprived of none of the advantages of the Society who adopts them, & represents in all place and occasion the deseased.
Art. 29. It is possible that once upon the spot of settlement some change shall be found necessary in the present regulations, or an adition of article, which may take place upon the proposition of one member of the Society when the two thirds & one shall give their asent, but in no case shall it be possible to attack or even put in deliberation the principle of Comunion, for ten years, nor derogate to the article 28.th
Art. 30. The deliberating thirds shall be counted in the following manner: the third of 5 will be 2- that of 8.= 3. that of 11.= 4. and so on when the number shall not give a just third
Art. 31 Every time that there shall be alterations to be made, or proposals that shall require to be put in deliberation, the object shall be determined by a Council of the Chiefs of family, in which shall be admitted with a Consultative voice the mothers of family & the young men of 20 years of age.

The present convenant in 31 articles shall be religiously observed by the contractants, we give for its execution & garantee, the free and sincere affirmation in the name of the Supreme Being, whose blessings we implore, and any age the generality of our present and future property wealth & chattel. Done & passed at the Chenit District of the Valley of the Lake of Joux, Canton of the Leman in Switzerland 30.the of April 1800.

Subscribed in the orriginal { D! Dufour, David Golay, Philipe Berney, Joseph Meylan, J. Pierre Boralley } each of them in the name of his own family

Transcription of "1801 Translation"

In the transcription below, the punctuation and spelling of the original manuscript have been preserved. However bold fonts, indents and paragraph spacing have been introduced to enhance readability.

The original document, in the collection of the Cincinnati History Library and Archives (Cincinnati Museum Center), is catalogued under the designator VF3762, and cannot be published without the permission of that institution.

The undersigned Relations & Friends have formed the following Contract.

Considering that it is in the order of Nature, that Fathers and Mothers should bring up their children in the fear God, by giving them an education whense they may draw the Ideas of morality & justice which distinguish the true christian, and to provide likewise to their temporal welfare, by endeavouring to procure them a settlement suitable to the honest man, who cultivating the earth fulfills the law assigned to him by the Creator, & avoids the snares continualy laid in Europe by the arts and commerce, against the virtue and moralite of their folowers

Considering that the convulsions & wars that are now raging in Europe seems to be an effet of the too considerable population, & are destructive of the right of proprety and have a tendency to destroy the notions of Justice that are the basis of Social happiness.

Considering that our Ideas of the social principles, <u>Liberty</u>. <u>Equality</u>. are established in the Constitution of the United States of America and powerfully maintained by the moral characters of its peopel.

Considering that to fulfill the ends of the Good Providence, the immense & firtile continent of the new world, must be settled & cultivated, & that those who have the wisdom & courage to quit the frivolous & dangerous resources that are now found in Switzerland shall be protected by him and loaded with his blessings.

Considering lastly, that this good Providence has already signalized his powerfull protection in the favour of our dear and worthy friend J.J. Dufour who since four years his cultivating the vine with succes in America, and to procure our future establishement or the close alliance that we form together: that consequently we must ascelerate as much as it lays in ouer power the execution of that entreprise by the acquisition of the land necessary for the colony &c. We agreed

Title 1. of the Departure order of the Journey & Cost thereof

Article 1st. Every chief of family shall supply the expences of his own family in proportion of the number of individuals and equipages, the whole calculated on equitable basis; the departure being fixed within the first fourtnight of November next

Art: 2d. Are not understood ~~in~~ private equipages all things that are destined to the establishment of the colony such as the shoots of fruit trees Vine &c. Tools and generally all what shall be destined to be put in common, all those objets must be boug. ht and transported in common.

Art. 3d. It is likewise understood that the waggons and horses for the road to the place of embarcation shall be found in common, & the losses that might result by selling them at the sea Port shall be suported by the community, according to the share they shall have therein

Art 4the There shall be nominated two members of the society that shall be specially charged with the Economy of the voyage, of the care and safety of the equipages, to keep the books of account to enquire exactly into the care and health of the travellers so as to procure them convenient diet; they may divide among themselves this stewardship so that every thing is carefully attended to

Art. 5the The mothers of family shall take care of the little children, & the young girls will second them with all their power. the Boys able to do any things shall be ~~under~~ at the orders of the two stewards

Art 6: As soon as the embarcation shall be arrested with the Capt. of the ship there shall be provided as many small provisions as may contribute to the ease of the Women & children at sea; there shall be made if necessary an agreemt with the Capt. so as to loge the sicks as conveniently as posible. the two Stewards shall be carefull that the sep shall be respected & order & decency exactly observed.

Title 2. Religion Education

Art. 7[the]. The Religion which we profess shall be maintained & transmitted to our children it rests upon the strict observation of the Evangelic Moral which shall serve as a Basis to the education of youth, the worship which we belive to be the most agreeable to God, is the practice of all the social virtues, but in order to ascertain and fortify those dispositions every Sunday shall be consecrated to render him our homages, thank him for his benefit and implore his blessings.

Art 8[the]. Till we are enabled to have a Minister apointed according the use of the Christian Church there shall be chose among us a Regent of the colony whose functions shall be

1. to say priers on Sundays and holly days. 2. to take care of the instruction of youth in the Christian morality, teach them writing. grammar cyphering &c. 3. to Preside the Tribunal of Family and to inspect the preservation of good moral

Art. 9[the]. The functions of the Regent shall not prevent him from his rural works, his lecons shall be given only in the dead season, when they shall keep him the place of the winter works.
he shall enjoy no other distinction but that to which his virtues & his zeal to fulfil the duties of his station will entitle him to.

Title 3. Properties

Art 10[the]. There can ~~not~~ be no division of properties before the terms of ten years from an entire communion as well of the lands as of their cultivation & productions.

Art 11 however, to maintain equity & emulation there shall be regulated herafter in what manner ever chief of family shall afterwards retire a just equivalent of what shall belong to him in proportion of his first funds for the acquisition of lands, the number of hands he had found for the culture, children and other persons suported by the society whom are unable to work

Art 12. As the purchase money is not considered by the society as its principal richess, when compared to the clearing and culture, the purchase money shall be compensated by bearing interest which shall be paid to every one or give credit in his account ~~and shall be~~ after it has been fixed when the value of said funds shall be know exactly.

Art 13 At the end of every year there shall be made a general evaluation of the work that shall be found by Every Chief of family or his partner as well by himself as by his children able to work or by the wormen he should have the means of finding after a deduction of the consumption of the individuals of his family not able to work

Art. 14 After this principle there shall be kept to each chief a open account where shall be specified what share he has in the settlement, by giving credit to him at the end of each year for the work he has done.

Art. 15. And as there may be some variation, & all the years may not be equal, those private account shall be kept open during ten years, at the end of which shall be determined ~~what~~ that share of each family

Art. 16. That the productions of the farm follow the same proportion, they shall be entirely employed to the improvement of the land, by paying the wages of hire hands, buildings, &c.

Art. 17. Our friend J. J. Dufour under whose auspice the present contract is to have its entire execution shall be invited by several Letters to make the acquisition of the Lands that are necesairy to the plan of the society as well as for the culture of the vine as to any other sort of culture that may be carried on by the Society, and the provisions for the sustainement of the colony till they may be obtained from our own cultivation.

Art. 18. He shall be invited to sanction the present contract & even indicate the changement~~s~~ he will think proper

Art 19. But in no instance shall he be able to alter the fundamental principle of comunity neither propose to any of the present members to receive him as workman under wages or forsake him alone by separating him from his family: His brother D.[1] Dufour binds himself formelly into the execution of this present article, & that under the reserve, & compensation stipulated by the precedents articles the complete Indivision of ten years can not be altered.

Title 4. Buildings. Dress & Diet

Art. 20. Untill the faculties of the Society be increased beyond the bare nesessairies of life, no buildings shall be undertaken but what shall be deemed indispensably necessary to the rural logings of the colony.

Art 21. The Dress shall be plain & modest, but cleanly kept uncleanliness being forbid_. ~~eae~~ each one owever shall find his own clothes,

Art. 22. The Diet shall be the same for all, frugality planiness, Economy and the greatest cleanliness must constitute the regiment of the Society.

Title 5. Feast and Diversions

Art 23. Beside Sunday and Holidays there shall be 4 great festivals in the year to be fixed afterward, which shall be the anniversary of the fourth greatest events arrived for the best of the Society, allthough the anniversary of the planting of the first vineyard shall be one of them; the Diversions shall always be preceded by thanksgiving to the Almighty by the Regent who afterwards shall order the diversions in a manner suitable to our circumstances - order and decency shall be regulerly observed.

Title 6. Tribunal of Family

Art. 24. It is to be understood that we submit ourselves entirely to the laws of the Country we are going to inhabit. & we beg the Allmighty to confirm us by an happy experience in the persuasion we are that never either Crime nor quarrel wil soil our Society and that the laws shall only serve us as a protectors.

Art. 25. In order to terminate all the little difference that might arise between the members of the Society, to maintain Decency as well as a Strict morality, likewise to repress Idleness & neglects there shall be a Tribunal of Family composed of four of the Eldest of the Society and presided by the Regent, besides two other members of the Society which the Defendant will have a right to chose, and by these means augment of two the number of his Juges

Art. 26. The tribunal of family shall pronounce arbitrarily upon all the cases mentioned in the precedent article, he may inflict Pains, & chastiments, such as to asign to the culprit a separate place & different victuals from the rest, the privation of the diversions for a limited time, and even pecuniary fines, which shall be destined to buy some Books useful to the youth.

Art. 27. Those on the contrairy who shall be distinguished by their love of work, their industry & activity, and exemplary behavior, shall receive encouragement from the Society such as the first seat at table, places of honour in the Diversions, crowns of honnour, nosegays on Sundays besides a present of some dres for their wearing on Sundays.

Title 7. Unforseen Events

Art 28. It is agreed that in the case of Death, either in the Journey or in the colony of a chief of family or his representant, the widow and orphans shall not be deprived of none of the advan-advantages of the Society who adopts them, & represents in all place and occasion the designated chief

Art 29. It is possible that once upon the spot of settlement some change shall be found necessary in the present regulations, or an adition of article, which may take place upon the proposition of one member of the Society when the two thirds & one shall give their asent, but in no case shall it be posible to attack or even put in deliberation the principle of Comunion for ten years, nor derogate to the article 28the.

Art. 30. The deliberating thirds shall be counted in the following manner: the third of 5 will be 2 that of 8. = 3. that of 11. = 4. and so on when the number shall not give a just third

Art 31 Every time that there shall be alterations to be made, or proposals that shall require to be put in deliberation, the object shall be determined by a Counsil of the Chiefs of family, in which shall be admitted with a consultative voice the mothers of family & the young men of 20 years of age.

The present convenant in 31 articles shall be religiously observed by the contractants, we give for its execution & garantee the free and sincere affirmation in the name of the Supreme Being, whose blesings we implore, and angage the generality of our present and future property, wealth & chattel. Done & pased at the Chenit District of the Valley of Lake of Joux, Canton of the Léman in Swiserland 30the of April 1800.

subscribed
in the
original

D^l. Dufour
David Golay
Philipe Berney
Joseph Meylan
J. Pierre Boralley

each in the name of his own family

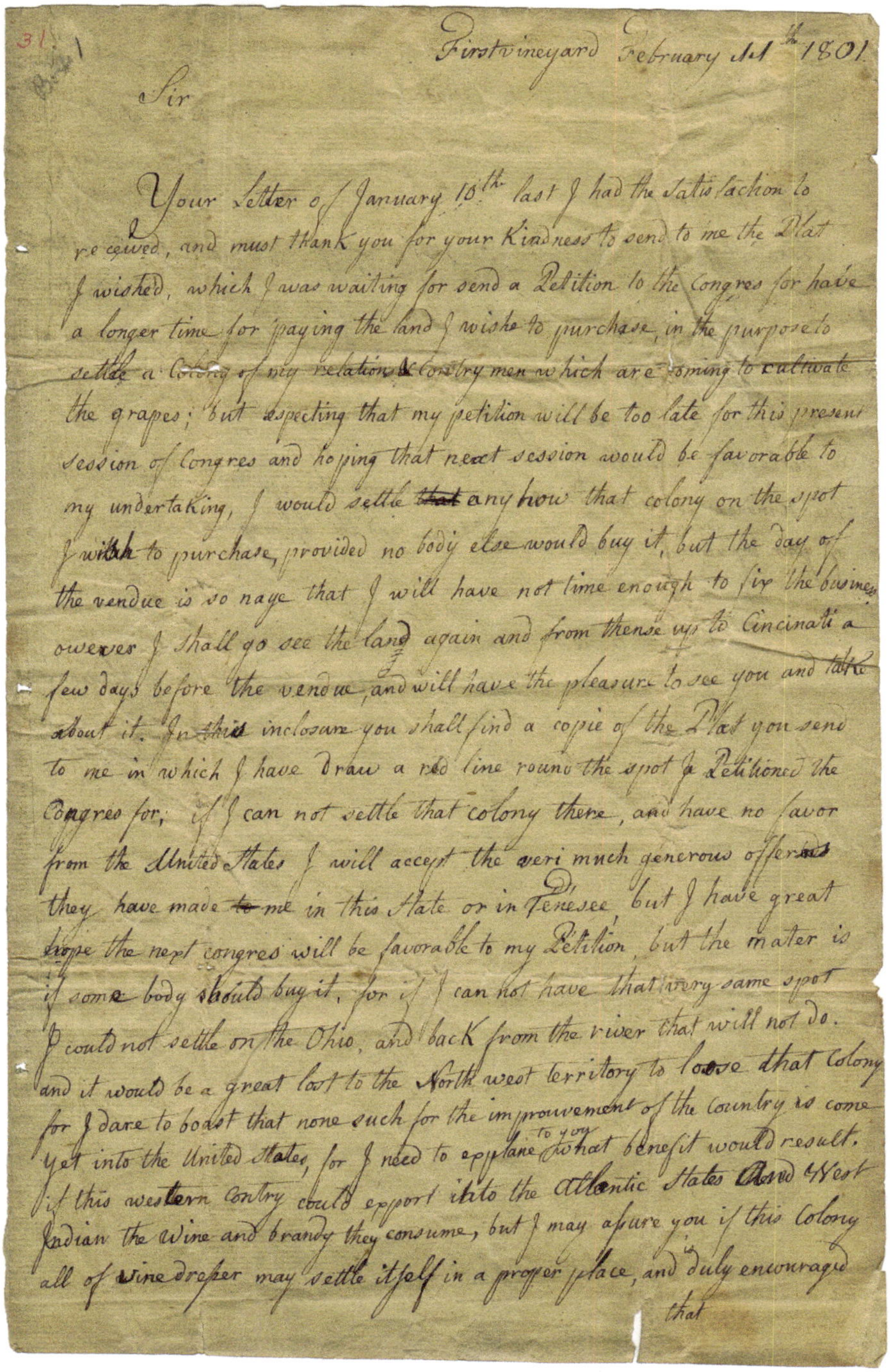

First vineyard February 1st 1801

Sir

Your Letter of January 15th last I had the satisfaction to received, and must thank you for your kindness to send to me the Plat I wished, which I was waiting for send a Petition to the Congres for have a longer time for paying the land I wishe to purchase, in the purpose to settle a colony of my relations & contry men which are coming to cultivate the grapes; but expecting that my petition will be too late for this present session of Congres and hoping that next session would be favorable to my undertaking, I would settle any how that colony on the spot I wish to purchase, provided no body else would buy it, but the day of the vendue is so naye that I will have not time enough to fix the business, owever I shall go see the land again and from thense up to Cincinati a few days before the vendue, and will have the pleasure to see you and talke about it. In this inclosure you shall find a copie of the Plat you send to me in which I have draw a red line round the spot I Petitioned the Congres for; if I can not settle that colony there, and have no favor from the United States I will accept the veri much generous offers they have made to me in this State or in Tenesee, but I have great hope the next congres will be favorable to my Petition, but the mater is if some body should buy it, for if I can not have that very same spot I could not settle on the Ohio, and back from the river that will not do. and it would be a great lost to the North west territory to loose that Colony for I dare to boast that none such for the improuvement of the country is come yet into the United States, for I need to explane to you what benefit would result if this western contry could eport into the Atlantic States and west Indian the wine and brandy they consume, but I may asure you if this Colony all of wine dreper may settle itself in a proper place, and duly encouraged

that

Fig. 10. Page 1, 1801 Letter, Mss VF3763
(courtesy of Cincinnati History Library and Archive)

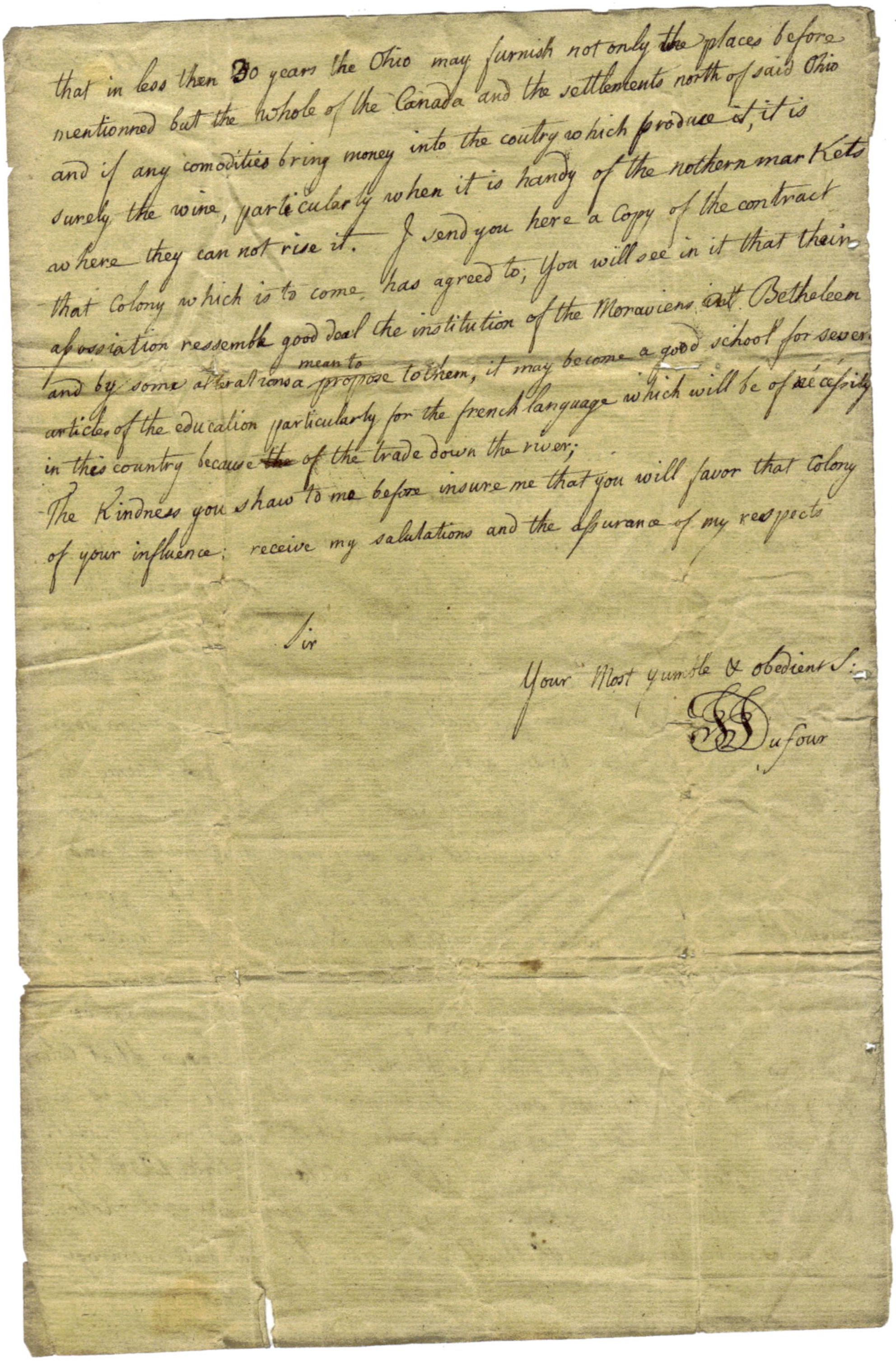

that in less then 30 years the Ohio may furnish not only the places before mentionned but the whole of the Canada and the settlements north of said Ohio and if any comodities bring money into the coutry which produce it, it is surely the wine, particularly when it is handy of the nothern markets where they can not rise it. — I send you here a copy of the contract that Colony which is to come, has agreed to; you will see in it that their apossiation ressembl good deal the institution of the Moraviens at Betheleem and by some alterations a propose to them, it may become a good school for sever articles of the education particularly for the french language which will be of necessity in this country because of the trade down the river;

The kindness you shaw to me before insure me that you will favor that Colony of your influence; receive my salutations and the assurance of my respects

Sir

Your Most yumble & obedient S:
Dufour

Fig. 11. Page 2, 1801 Letter, Mss VF3763
(courtesy of Cincinnati History Library and Archive)

Transcription of "1801 Letter"

In the following line-by-line transcription of Jean Jaques Dufour's 1801 Letter, the punctuation and spelling of the original manuscript are preserved. Words and letters within brackets [ ] have been added by the transcriber.

The original document, in the collection of the Cincinnati History Library and Archives (Cincinnati Museum Center), is catalogued under the designator VF3762, and cannot be published without the permission of that institution.

$$\text{First vineyard} \quad \text{February } 11^{th} \text{ 1801}$$

Sir

Your letter of January 10th last I had the satisfaction to
received, and must thank you for your kindness to send to me the Plat
I wished, which I was waiting for [in order to] send a Petition to the Congres for have
a longer time for paying the land I wishe to purchase, in the purpose to
settle a Colony of my relations & country men which are coming to cultivate
the grapes; but expecting that my petition will be too late for this present
session of Congres and hoping that next session would be favorable to
my undertaking, I would settle any how that colony on the spot
I wish to purchase, provided no body else would buy it, but the day of
the vendue is so naye that I will have not time enough to fix the business
owever I shall go see the land again and from thense up to Cincinati a
few days before the vendue, and will have the pleasure to see you and talk
about it. In this inclosure you shall find a copie of the Plat you send
to me in which I have draw a red line round the spot I Petitioned the
Congres for; if I can not settle that colony there, and have no favor
from the United States I will accept the veri much generous offerred
they have made to me in this State or in Tenesee, but I have great
hope the next congres will be favorable to my Petition, but the mater is
if some body should buy it, for if I can not have that very same spot
I could not settle on the Ohio, and back from the river that will not do
and it would be a great lost to the North west territory to loose that Colony
for I dare to boast that none such for the improvement of the country is come
yet into the United States, for I need to explane to you what benefit would result
if this western contry could export into the Atlantic States And West
Indian the wine and brandy they consume, but I may assure you if this Colony
all of vinedresser may settle itself in a proper place, and is duly encouraged
$$\hspace{20em}\text{that}$$

---

that in less then 40 30 years the Ohio may furnish not only the places before
mentioned but the whole of the Canada and the settlements north of said Ohio
and if any comodities bring money into the coutry which produse it, it is
surely the wine, particularly when it is handy of the northern markets
where they can not rise it. I send you here a copy of the contract
that Colony which is to come has agreed to; you will see in it that their
assossiation ressemble good deal the institution of the Moraviens at Betheleem
and by some alterations a mean to propose to them, it may become a good school for sever[al]

articles of the education particularly for the french language which will be of necessity in this country because ~~the~~ of the trade down the river;
The Kindness you shaw to me before insure me that you will favor that colony of your influence;   receive my salutations and the assurance of my respects

Sir

Your most yumble & obedient S

JJDufour

Comments

1. Both the 1801 Translation and the 1801 Letter appear to be in the same hand, apparently that of Jean Jaques Dufour.

2. It is safe to conclude that the 1801 Translation was made by a native French speaker. Spellings such as "effet," "entreprise," and "objets" are unlikely to have been introduced by a native English speaker.

From the time of his arrival in the U.S. on about August 12, 1796, Jean Jaques Dufour's command of English was at least sufficient to engage in simple business transactions. Among these was the purchase of a French-English dictionary in Baltimore on September 22, 1796; about a year later in St. Louis he added a second dictionary and an English grammar to his library. **(13)** His daybook entries indicate that in 1796-1797 many of his interactions were with French-speaking merchants. In 1798, as he establishes himself in Kentucky, his English-speaking contacts increase markedly. As early as January 10, 1798 Dufour published a very lengthy and detailed proposal in English in the *Kentucky Gazette*, a Lexington newspaper. **(14)** More generally, one sees that he navigated easily and unabashedly across America's physical, linguistic, and social landscape, never hesitating to address anyone about his most beloved hopes.

3. If one compares Dufour's 1801 Translation with the original 1800 Compact, there are a few variations. The most notable differences occur when the colony is defining its relationship to Jean Jaques Dufour himself.

As will be discussed later, many of the articles under Title 3 are awkwardly worded, both in the original (1800 Compact) and in the 1801 Translation. Here the settlers were grappling with a complex problem. For the moment, let's simply note that Title 3 is called "Acquisitions, Work, Common and Privately Held Property" in the 1800 Compact, but merely "Properties" in the 1801 Translation. With that, Dufour was zeroing in on what was everyone's principal concern: how would a large tract of land initially held in common be subsequently divided among several families?

In particular, the two versions of Article 19 reflect opposing anxieties. Dufour is concerned that he will be treated differently, perhaps as a mere employee or agent of the Colony. The colonists, on the other hand, are afraid that Dufour might separate himself and his siblings from the provisions of the compact, and Daniel Dufour must therefore pledge his determination that this will not happen.

Also, on an issue less fraught, Dufour refrains from describing all but one of the four feast days mandated under the compact in Article 23. For him the signal day was that on which he first installed a vine in American soil. He doubted, perhaps, that an American official would be overly impressed by the colony's reverence for their own departure and "embracing" dates.

4. I detect, both from the translation and the letter (not to mention hindsight), that Dufour was writing in some haste and with urgency. He did not waste many moments consulting his dictionaries and grammar textbook, nor did he have a native English speaker review his translation for its spelling and intelligibility. His main point in submitting the compact was to demonstrate the earnestness and worthiness of the Swiss colonists. In a few weeks (on April 1, 1801) the Federal Land Office would be offering for sale lands that included the Indiana shoreline of the Ohio River and the very site Dufour was most desirous of obtaining for the Colony. By then the *Voodsop*, bearing the colonists and their cargo of perishable vine cuttings, would be midway across the Atlantic and daily expected in Virginia. He hadn't a moment to lose.

5. I value the 1801 Letter that accompanied the 1801 Translation on several grounds. I think because Dufour is writing quickly we are hearing –as nearly as one can– his voice, his French-inflected English. By contrast, his January 1798 letter in the *Gazette* and 1801 Petition to Congress **(14, 15)**, also in English, are more crafted and polished, and may have received the attentions of an editor or advisor.

Secondly, I was both gratified and perplexed to read "...*you will see in it that their assossiation ressemble good deal the institution of the Moraviens at Betheleem.*" Upon first encountering the 1800 Compact, I had questioned whether the colonists, in framing their agreement, were following the example of another Swiss consortium or band of settlers bound for the New World. Was it customary for Swiss Protestants to draft covenants for such ventures? In the opinion of at least one expert, it was not – at least not at this early date. **(16)** And, in my own feeble attempt to access 18th century French and Swiss founding documents, I had not uncovered a counterpart to the 1800 Compact. But then again, I was seeking a European model for it. Thus, to read that the Moravian Community in Bethlehem, Pennsylvania may have inspired a group of Swiss vine growers was indeed a revelation.

To digress briefly: the Moravian Church ("Unitas Fratum") had its origins in a central European religious reform movement that pre-dated Luther's by more than a century. Its heterodox views insured that its adherents would face reprisals and persecution during the 16th-17th centuries, almost to the point of extirpation. In the 18th century a revived Moravian Church undertook an organized migration from Saxony to British North America, establishing a congregation first in Savannah, Georgia (1735) and another soon afterwards in Pennsylvania. From 1741-1762, the Moravians at Bethlehem, Pennsylvania lived communally under an arrangement termed the General Economy, or "Oeconomy." In 1754 eight precepts regulating the Oeconomy were promulgated in a "Brotherly Agreement," and in 1762 a superseding Brotherly Agreement concluded the era of economic communalism. **(17)** Not rigidly doctrinaire, the community tended to resolve issues on an ad-hoc basis, relying more on the instructions of its elders and the "guidance of the Savior" than upon a founding document. Communalism had not been an end unto itself, but simply the most efficient means of supporting missionary outreach to native Americans, African slaves, and newly-arrived Europeans. **(18)**

Initial investigations at the Moravian Archives in Pennsylvania failed to uncover any evidence that Jean Jaques Dufour had visited Bethlehem. Specifically, "The Bethlehem Diary" and the guest register of Bethlehem's only public inn were consulted to no avail. However, this does not rule out the possibility of an informal visit being made by Dufour at some time between 1796–1800. According to archivist Thomas McCullough (pers. comm.) the Bethlehem Moravians attempted to start a winery in the 1750s but were unsuccessful. Certainly, in the late 1790s there would have been no vineyards at Bethlehem to attract Dufour's attention. Addressing another question, McCullough explained that in the 1790s the Brotherly Agreement was not a published document in general circulation: it therefore seems unlikely that Jean Jaques Dufour ever saw a copy of it. In truth, there is little similarity between the Brotherly Agreements (1754 and 1762) and the 1800 Compact. [The eight articles of the 1754 Brotherly Agreement appear in Sessler **(19)** and the 1762 Brotherly Agreement may be viewed online. **(20)**] In any case, the origin, mission, and scale of the Moravian community at Bethlehem was of an entirely different order than that of the Swiss colonists, or so it now seems to us.

If so, what are we to make of Dufour's allusion to the "Moraviens at Betheleem?" At the very least, either he or someone among the colonists had gained a favorable impression of the devout, industrious Moravians, even if that impression had been gained through hearsay rather than personal acquaintance. Secondly, the Moravian model would have been reassuring to the Swiss colonists who were planning to begin as a communal society and then transition to private land ownership. Finally, Dufour surely thought that by raising the example of the Moravians, he was communicating to federal officials that the Swiss promised to be as upright and productive as that exemplary group.

Fig. 12. Bethlehem, Pennsylvania in 1784. Two decades of communalism enabled the Moravians to quickly establish themselves in Pennsylvania's wilderness and create a small city filled with commercial enterprises whose profits were directed towards the support of itinerant preachers and missions in North America, South America and the Caribbean. The speed with which this group had transformed their surroundings would have encouraged the Swiss in respect to their own enterprise, and perhaps was viewed by them as an instance wherein Providence had indeed intervened on the behalf of pious agriculturalists. ["Bethlehem, Pennsylvania." 1784. Watercolor on paper. Artist: Nicholas Garrison. Courtesy of the Moravian Archives, Bethlehem, Pennsylvania.]

DISCUSSION

It seems that the 1800 Compact was an instrument devised by the Swiss colonists to address their very particular and immediate circumstances. Most likely, they were not intentionally mimicking any earlier covenant or contract. Furthermore, while the Compact helped to organize the colonists before their departure, it may not have governed them significantly after their arrival in North America. The document's ultimate value to them resided elsewhere.

Presumably the Compact lost much of its authority when two of its signers, Philippe Berney and Joseph Meylan, either chose or were compelled to remain in Switzerland. We don't know if their replacements (François Louis Siebenthal, Philippe Bettens, and Jean Daniel Morerod) signed a later version of the agreement. If so, it may be that Article 10 (deemed unchangeable under Article 29) was then revised along the lines urged by Daniel Dufour:

...I find there is a large change to be made and some articles to add. First, the term of ten years without being able to break or divide the Society's property seems too long to me; our hands would all be tied. Boralley is of the same opinion, so I am going write to La Vallée to invite our friends who have signed to consent that the term be reduced to six years instead of ten. You can count on it. **(1800 Lettre)**

Secondly, it appears that many of the provisions under Title 3 were disregarded once feet were on the ground in America. Immediately upon the colonists' arrival in Kentucky (in July 1801) Dufour contracted with his siblings to share in the labor he owed to the Kentucky Vineyard Society. **(21)** This arrangement ultimately delayed their locating to Indiana for several years and appears to be precisely a situation that the drafters of the 1800 Compact had sought to prevent through Article 19. Next, six months later and while still encamped at First Vineyard in Kentucky, the colonists agreed to divide the Indiana tract obtained under the 1802 congressional act into equal portions of 193 80/100 acres. **(6)** Thus, there never would be a moment when communal land ownership was tried, nor was any effort made to calculate the relative inputs of each family and to divide the land accordingly. Given the opaque wording of the Compact and the colonists' radical change in circumstances, how such an assessment was to be fairly made may have escaped comprehension, leading the settlers to abandon the idea altogether.

However other provisions of the Compact *could* have been followed. It's likely that living quarters, harvested produce, meals, supplies, tools, and labor were indeed shared during the first years in Indiana, given the speed with which vineyards came into production. **(22)** It's reasonable to assume that celebrations and religious observances were communal events. A memory of Daniel Dufour presiding over Sunday worship services perhaps affords us a glimpse of someone acting in the role of "Regent." **(23)**

If we arbitrarily designate children aged 4-16 as being of school age, then there were four potential scholars aboard the *Voodsop* in April 1801: Susanne Marguerite Dufour (age 15); Jean David Dufour (12); Pierre Daniel Boralley (10); and Susanne Marie Boralley (7). But by 1803 when the Swiss families moved to Indiana, none of these four were present: the two youngest Dufours remained at First Vineyard in Kentucky, while the Boralley children accompanied their newly-widowed mother to Garrard County, Kentucky. However, Charlotte Bettens, who did move to Indiana with her parents, had attained the age of 5 and was now of school age. Other signers of the 1800 Compact (Jaques David Golay, Philippe Berney, and Joseph Meylan) would likely have contributed more students had they followed their original plans: we know for certain that the Golays had at least five children of school age in 1803. Due to these shortfalls, the colonial school envisioned by the Compact was not expressly realized, so far as one can tell. This, combined with Jean Jaques Dufour's prolonged sojourn in Switzerland (1806-1816) and the arrival of many more settlers (Swiss and non-Swiss), further diminished any possibility that a coherently ordered colony in the style of the Moravians, Harmonists, Shakers, etc. would materialize in New Switzerland.

~~~

The Kentucky Vineyard Society was very much the creation of Jean Jaques Dufour, albeit one inspired by a similar enterprise in Pennsylvania. **(24)** Having toured the Mid-Atlantic states, the Ohio River Valley, and the Mississippi River from its junction with the Ohio River south to Cape Girardeau, Dufour returned east in 1797 greatly enlightened about the country's geography, not to mention its very lean history of grape-growing. Arriving in Lexington, Kentucky on October 29, Dufour now had a plan in view. Over the next two months, he canvassed and buttonholed many of the town's merchants, politicians, and leading lights, sharing his views on the untold potential for viticulture in their state. Given that Lexington's residential population was then about 1700 **(25),** he may well have spoken to almost everyone. By January 1798 he had garnered sufficient encouragement and kindly advice to pen a letter "to the citizens of Kentucky," providing a highly detailed prospectus for a shareholder-owned vineyard. **(14)** Within weeks the Kentucky Vineyard Society was formed and in October a Jessamine County site called "First Vineyard" was purchased. During this period Dufour wrote to his family on at least three occasions: on July 14, 1798 from Philadelphia; on July 19, 1798 from New York City **(26)**; and on July 23, 1798 from New York City **(1800 lettre)**, no doubt acquainting them with his plans.

If Dufour had come to America to establish a colony of Swiss vine growers, why was he taking this detour - one that would require his undivided attention and diligence on behalf of the Kentucky investors? No doubt his letters and journals, and those of his relatives, would have enlightened us had these survived. Instead, the best one can do is to generate reasonable hypotheses, and here I'll submit three. First, the idea of a Swiss colony may not even have been conceived before 1799. Or, if a colony was indeed being planned, the political turmoil in Switzerland in 1798-1799 may have engendered a pause - the duration of which could not be predicted. Under this scenario, Dufour would not have anticipated the imminent arrival of his relatives and associates. Or this: Dufour may have thought that First Vineyard could serve as a nucleus around which the Swiss would build a wider enterprise. Perhaps the colonists would become owner/shareholders themselves.

A close reading of Daniel Dufour's 1800 Lettre and Jean Jaques Dufour's 1801 letter to Thomas Jefferson **(2)** allows us to suspect that all three hypotheses may apply. Dufour most likely departed Switzerland knowing that his family intended to join him, while other parties were awaiting with interest his reports. In July 1798 he could write to his relatives with some enthusiasm regarding the Kentucky Vineyard Society, perhaps appealing for their active participation while also recommending that they purchase land along the Ohio River in the Northwest Territory. Events unfolding in Vaud delayed their immediate assent, but by June 1800, the Dufours and four other families would commit to joining forces in America, only <u>not</u> in Kentucky and only <u>if</u> the group were to form a communal economy during the initial stages of settlement. One or both of these conditions may have surprised Jean Jaques Dufour (not to mention the colonists' command that he procure the initial financing for the venture).

He portrayed his dilemma to Jefferson **(2)** in this manner:
"... the place that seemed to me to be the first choice is on the banks of the Ohio... in the lands that Congress possesses and that are to be sold this spring... But I cannot buy these lands under the terms of the law for lack of means, which the war, the revolution in my own country, and my great travels have practically annihilated, as well as having prevented my family from coming to join me as had been agreed. <u>That is why I had almost renounced a foundation on the Ohio</u> <u>and, so</u> <u>as not to have come for nothing at all, two years ago I planted a vineyard on the banks of the</u>

Kentucky, which promises to be a great success, and the reputation of which having reached as far as Switzerland, I engaged four great respectable families to join mine to import vines into this country. They order me to buy them some land, not knowing that I no longer have the means, having placed the small funds that remained to me to maintain the establishment where I am, which was going to fail due to the failure of the subscribers to pay. [emphasis added]

While much of Dufour's thought process must remain veiled, some facts are plain. Jean Jaques Dufour was as much a missionary as any Moravian, only his goal was to initiate an agrarian society thriving amid ripening vines and flowering orchards. Many of his surviving letters penned in this period brim with a visionary promise that the Ohio Valley would soon rival the Rhone or Rhine valleys as a wine making district. To this purpose he had dedicated his life. Constructing vineyards, tending vines, and winemaking were second nature to him. No wonder that after two droughty years in America, Dufour longed to be standing among his own flourishing vines and witnessing their growing bounty. The support he had received from the likes of Henry Clay, John Bradford and Senator John Brown was in the nature of Providence itself, and one could not be idle before an enterprise so blessed. This *was* the favored moment. Nonetheless his haste in procuring vines unsettled even the Kentucky shareholders. They had anticipated that he would travel to Europe to purchase cuttings, and that two years would necessarily pass before an infant vineyard was underway in Kentucky. Instead, within eleven months Dufour had procured 22,000 scions (of recent European origin, or so he thought) from several sites in the eastern U.S. and had planted his first American vineyard. **(27)** Another example of Dufour's surpassing enthusiasm may be detected in the fact that although the colonists initially had asked him to obtain 4,000-5,000 acres in the Northwest Territory (see 1800 Lettre), he instead petitioned for 7,000. **(3,4)**

At first glance, Dufour's choices appear problematic both for the Swiss colonists and the Kentucky Vineyard Society. We see hints of this not only in Daniel Dufour's letter to his brother (1800 Lettre) and in the wording of Article 19, but perhaps also in the very framing of the 1800 Compact itself. Conceivably one of its purposes was to impose some restraint on Jean Jaques Dufour. For their part, the Kentucky Vineyard Society made clear that while the emigres could take temporary respite at First Vineyard, they were not entitled to its commercial profits. **(28)** According to Jean Jaques Dufour, his Kentucky backers had been greatly disappointed to learn that the colonists were going to apply their viticultural skills in the Northwest Territory rather than in Kentucky. **(29)**

In retrospect, we can see that the creation of First Vineyard was not as out of joint as it first appears. From the colonists' perspective, the site provided shelter and sustenance until they obtained their own land. They had arrived not only penniless, but actually in debt to a Lexington merchant, Lewis Sanders, who paid for their passage from Pittsburgh to Kentucky. **(30, 31)** During the year they resided at First Vineyard, the emigres gained their footing, viewed their prospective homeland, and had time to equilibrate and to refine their plans. In the meanwhile, to the benefit of the Kentucky Vineyard Society, the colonists assisted with the maintenance and expansion of the vineyard, and they definitely would have installed their European vine cuttings – the ones so much desired by the Kentucky investors. Most significantly, First Vineyard functioned as a test plot. It was here that all concerned witnessed the dismal failure of most of the vines, but also the plucky survival and promise of at least two varieties, whose next home was to be in New Switzerland.

~~~

In recounting the story of Vevay and its Swiss colonists, we are always handicapped by the absence of first-hand accounts in the form of letters or journals. This applies especially to the 1791-1801 decade, and most crucially to the experiences of the future immigrants while yet in Switzerland. I am fairly confident that investigations in Vaud would yield some rewards. At the very least, one could document the general impact of an intensifying political crisis upon the citizens of Montreux, Vevey, and in the Vallée du Lac de Joux. Some of the critical events punctuating this interval were the Bernese suppression of Vaudois republicans (1791); establishment of the Lémanic Republic (January, 1798); the incursion into Vaud by French troops (January 28, 1798); formation of the Helvetic Republic (April, 1798); the French occupation of Switzerland (1798-1802); outbreak of the War of the Second Coalition (1798) with major conflict centered in Switzerland (1799); Napoleon's advance through Vaud (May, 1800); and multiple uprisings leading to the collapse of the Helvetic Republic in February 1803. **(32)**

In a July 1800 letter published in the Kentucky Gazette **(33)**, Jean Jaques Dufour wrote:

...I shall only observe, that when I procured the Vines at New-York and Philadelphia, instead of going for them in Europe, I did not so much consult my own convenience, as the advantages of the [Kentucky Vineyard] society. I had concerns in Switzerland of much more consequence to me than any thing of a private nature here; especially as my brother who had charge of my affairs in that country had joined the army. It is fortunate however that I did not go, for had I have gone, I should not have been able to have returned.

Two original documents owned by Christy Williams **(34,35)** attest to Daniel Dufour's enlistment into the l'Armée Helvétique as a "Commissaire des Guerres" on April 10, 1799. Lacking additional information, we cannot determine whether Daniel was acting from patriotism, economic necessity or strategic considerations. By 1799, Swiss communities were being compelled to provide the French army with men as well as revenue in the form of mandatory loans. Lausanne for example yielded 9,000 men at this time. **(36)** If Daniel (age 34) preferred to serve under Swiss rather than French authority, he may have enlisted proactively. In any case, his absence would have imposed a hardship on his family, given that the next-oldest male (Jean François) was only 15-16 years old in 1799. Also caught up in the vortex of war was Jean Daniel Morerod. Most likely as a conscripted or volunteer laborer (as opposed to a military inductee), Morerod was awarded the grueling task of hauling artillery over a wintery Alpine pass in May 1800, prior to the Battle of Morengo. **(37)**

A Jaques-David Golay descendant has documented the pivotal 1798-1799 years in the vicinity of Le Chenit, during which Golay, his father Isaac Philippe Golay, and Philippe Berney actively participated in the climactic events that toppled the Bernese oligarchy, only to witness the Helvetic Republic replicate nearly every misdeed of the previous regime. At the turn of the 19th century famine, war, repressive governance, and the extortions of the French army had brought the local economy to a standstill. A prosperous businessman, Golay watched one enterprise that he managed (the industrial forges at Brassus) fold through judicial malfeasance. **(38)**

Other indications that the emigres had suffered economically can be gleaned from Jean Jaques Dufour's 1801 and 1802 letters to Thomas Jefferson and his 1801 Petition to Congress:

...But I cannot buy these lands under the terms of the law for lack of means, which the war, the revolution in my own country, and my great travels have practically annihilated, as well as having prevented my family from coming to join me as had been agreed. **(2)**

...That this Colony having in common with your Petitioner sustained many heavy losses of property by the late war and Revolution in their native country... **(15)**

...but because of the war that corporation broke up and only a small number of settlers came. **(3)**

Still, had there been no war or if its impacts had been less severe, it may nonetheless have been incumbent upon the Dufours and their compatriots to contemplate emigration to America. A force more implacable than imperial conflict was at work: the pressure that increasing population and growing wealth were applying to the price of land. Political and technological revolutions were engendering a new monied class comprised of industrialists, global traders, merchants, bankers, generals, magistrates and other high-ranking officials. These individuals almost inevitably sought to anchor their status through land ownership. Hereditary small holders like Jean Jaques Dufour, Sr., hoping to provide their heirs with a sufficiency of land, were increasingly priced out of the market. **(16)** Significantly, this pressure was being felt at the very moment when the United States was opening its western territories for settlement. In chronic need of revenue to pay its war debts, the U.S. government gradually abandoned its practice of carving out large tracts for speculators to market and, under the Harrison Land Act (May 10, 1800), began selling small parcels directly to settlers.

Thus we see that much is converging here. Parents, whose duty it is to secure the future of their children, are unable to do so because of increasing population, escalating land values, extreme political instability, economic distress, and war. Rudderless Switzerland, flanked on either side by warring giants Austria and France, appears unlikely to survive the current conflict. Was it not providential that the United States, in opening its western lands to new settlement, should offer a remedy at just this moment?

~~~

While religion may not have been the impetus, it could well have provided the footing from which the Swiss colonists enacted their leap of faith. To forsake one's homeland and relations, embark on a one-way voyage, and risk a family's entire patrimony: this is a transition more radical than many of us are ever likely to make, and one that may require either a profound faith, philosophy, or guiding conviction to even contemplate.

Given their birthplace, we may safely assume that the signers of the 1800 Compact were, in every case, Reformed Protestants. But even that designation embraces a universe of viewpoints, some of them quite divergent. Still, in the following extracts from the compact, we can isolate two recurring themes that may have been the most potent elements of the colonists' shared theology.

Considering that it is in the order of nature that fathers and mothers take greatest care to raise their children in the fear of God, giving them an education from which they can draw the concepts of morality and justice that characterize true Christians, while at the same time providing for their temporal well-being, by seeking to procure for them a condition worthy of a virtuous person who, <u>by working to cultivate the earth, fulfills the goal of the Creator and avoids the traps that art, industry, and commerce in Europe</u> set ceaselessly to spoil the virtue and morality of those who indulge in them…

… Considering that, in order <u>to fulfill the will of Providence, the immense and fertile New World will be populated and cultivated</u>, and those with the wisdom and courage to leave the currently frivolous and dangerous state of affairs in Switzerland <u>will be protected and blessed by heaven.</u>

Considering, finally, that this <u>divine Providence has already shown its powerful protection</u> of our dear and worthy friend Jean Jaques Dufour … [emphases added]

First, they share a belief in a purposeful and protecting God, a divine Providence that is ordering creation towards a specific end. The concept of Providence varied significantly throughout Protestantism, and the signers of the 1800 Compact may be expressing a more liberal notion than would normally have been admitted under Calvinism (although the compact's wording does leave room for several interpretations). The colonists appear to suggest that the virtuous should seek to harmonize their lives with their Creator's intentions. A strict Calvinist, on the other hand, would reject the notion that humans can, of their own will, cooperate in God's inscrutable, unalterable plan or that "Providence" will afford protection based on one's actions. I'd submit that while Calvinism might dampen the ardor for radical action, a more expansive view of Providence could propel believers to take great risks.

Secondly, the writers firmly believe that an agrarian life tends to be godlier than an urban existence based on industry or commerce. Not a religious scholar, I'm unable to trace this physiocratic stance to a particular strain of Christianity and can merely point to its prominence in the 1800 Compact. But surely if one held this belief, then the unsettled realms of North America *would* seem an ideal refuge from the all the ills of 18th – early 19th century Europe.

Although the 1800 Compact offers a glimpse into the mindset of the Swiss colonists, the epistles penned by one of their elders are perhaps more illuminating. The parent of the Dufours, Jean Jaques Dufour, Sr., did not immigrate with his children, apparently due to his advanced age and weak health. According to Knox **(39)** it was his custom to write sermons addressed to his children in America, and indeed two of these have survived due to their being published, posthumously, in a missionary publication. **(40, 41)** One letter dates from 1804, the other from 1805. Both are well worth examining in their entirety, as they reflect upon situations that the settlers were encountering in America. But for the purpose of detecting the particular religious stripe of the Dufours, the following three passages are a useful sample:

[I am] a laborer, a vinedresser, who never had any other instructor but my late father; who have never studied any other book than my Bible; who have never been taught the rules of elocution. My language is altogether simple and rustic... **(40)**

God has exhibited in his word all that we ought to know, to understand, to believe, and to practice, that we may secure our true happiness both in this world and the world to come. Whatever men wish to add is erroneous, and those who wish to retrench are impious. **(40)**

...to confirm yourselves more and more in this purifying faith, and so become instruments in advancing the glory of God and hastening the complete introduction of his kingdom; which, as I hope, is about to commence in your country, sooner than in Europe. Since the constitution of your government is happy, nothing then will equal your joy, especially if you have contributed ever so little to its introduction. **(41)**

If I am not mistaken, the language of the first passage evinces a pietistic outlook, one that favors a personal, experiential Christianity over a faith closely ordered by clerics, doctrine, scholasticism, and ritual. The second quotation, assigning all authority to the Holy Writ, is consistent with the teaching of Ulrich Zwingli and other prominent Swiss reformers. In the third passage, Dufour is expressing a peculiar millennial belief, one that can be time-transgressive (i.e. that permits the kingdom of God to arrive earlier in America, later in Europe): with this, I'm at a loss to identify a particular source. Nonetheless from this collation, and from the overriding earnestness of his letters, Jean Jaques Dufour, Sr. emerges as an exceedingly devout man, and truly representative of a generation that came of age during the European equivalent of the first Great Awakening. Whether his beliefs were fully shared by his offspring cannot be known, but there is little doubt that Jean Jaques Dufour, Jr. inherited his father's zeal and steadfastness, even if he directed those qualities toward a tangential purpose.

~~~

Where father and son may have been in perfect alignment was in their reverence for viticulture. While dutifully parsing the father's sermon of July 1804 -a Protestant text to its very core- I was very much surprised to read this:

You know the advice of the Abbot of the vinedressers of Vevey: "Ora et labora." Pray while you work. It is necessary then to pray and labor to acquire things necessary for the body; it is equally necessary to pray and labor to obtain food for the immortal soul." **(40)**

Who, I wondered, was this anachronistic and unlikely Abbot? Who in Vaud (ca. 1800) was so brazenly quoting St. Benedict and memorializing a key tenet of Catholic monasticism?

My mystification would only be dispelled months later when I was researching the various museums in Vaud that might hold in their collections 18th century documents relevant to this study. One such museum in Vevey is maintained by the "Confrérie des Vignerons de Vevey," a society dedicated to the continuation and improvement of vine-growing and winemaking in the district. Although the group can document its existence as far back as 1618, the very fact that its chief officer is titled "Abbot" and its members (until recently) "Brothers" or "Monks," not to mention that a patron saint is still evoked (St. Urban), suggests that the organization formed in an earlier, Catholic age. While the rest of Europe was racked by violent sectarian strife in the 17th century, the Confrérie placidly continued to elect its Abbots and to scrutinize the health of Vevey's precious vineyards. By the late 18th century, the brotherhood's membership included almost one fourth of Vevey's male population and its celebratory parades and festivals were beginning to attract wider attention. **(42)**

The fact that the elder Dufour was perfectly comfortable in evoking the Abbot, and through him St. Benedict, and that the society held onto its Catholic symbols so manifestly, goes beyond being a delightful eccentricity. It conveys, I think, the deep history of viticulture in that region, and the very strong cultural and religious importance that the Vaudois attached to it. Whether as Catholics or Protestants, they believed that the careful tending of vines was a godly labor.

Fig. 13. The Abbot of La Confrérie des Vignerons de Vevey, ca. 1791. His staff of office is patterned on the crosier traditionally associated with bishops, abbots, and other high-ranking clerics in the Catholic church. Another important artifact preserved by the Confrérie is a chalice decorated with medals commemorating each Abbot from 1618 to the present day. [Courtesy of La Confrérie des Vignerons, Vevey, Switzerland]

~~~

Before taking leave of the Swiss colonists and their compact, let us now reconsider the meaning of their words and actions. Someone among them insured that the document was safely passed down to us and regarded it as important. The 1800 Compact had not been fully followed or enacted, but it had enabled the Swiss to envision themselves in America. They placed their faith in one another, in Jean Jaques Dufour, and in Providence and acted accordingly. The first generation of immigrants would honor their promises made to Congress, and indeed succeeded in establishing the first commercial winegrowing region in the U.S. against terrible odds. In his petition to Congress **(15)** Jean Jaques Dufour vowed "to use every exertion by his example to render the Cultivation of the Vine familiar to the people of the United States," a pledge he magnificently fulfilled by publishing *The American Vine-Dresser's Guide* in 1826 - a comprehensive tome penned in his own labored English and offered with a generous heart. These examples set by the colonists, and their gifts bequeathed to us, remain worthy of respect.

Having been reminded by Knox **(43)** and John and James Butler **(44)** of a scene preserved in Dufour memory -that of Jean Jaques Dufour, Sr. bidding farewell to his children by reading Psalm 90- I recently attempted to re-engage with that text and to view it through the perspective of the father and his departing children. Previously, when as a young Dufour descendant my attention had been directed to this psalm, all I could perceive in it were its references to wrath, anger, death, and destruction. I found neither succor nor beauty in it, although now I can detect at least a trace.

[1] Lord, thou hast been our dwelling place in all generations.
[2] Before the mountains were brought forth, or ever thou hadst formed the earth and the world, even from everlasting to everlasting, thou art God.
[3] Thou turnest man to destruction; and sayest, Return, ye children of men.
[4] For a thousand years in thy sight are but as yesterday when it is past, and as a watch in the night.
[5] Thou carriest them away as with a flood; they are as a sleep: in the morning they are like grass which groweth up.
[6] In the morning it flourisheth, and groweth up; in the evening it is cut down, and withereth.
[7] For we are consumed by thine anger, and by thy wrath are we troubled.
[8] Thou hast set our iniquities before thee, our secret sins in the light of thy countenance.
[9] For all our days are passed away in thy wrath: we spend our years as a tale that is told.
[10] The days of our years are threescore years and ten; and if by reason of strength they be fourscore years, yet is their strength labour and sorrow; for it is soon cut off, and we fly away.
[11] Who knoweth the power of thine anger? even according to thy fear, so is thy wrath.
[12] So teach us to number our days, that we may apply our hearts unto wisdom.
[13] Return, O LORD, how long? and let it repent thee concerning thy servants.
[14] O satisfy us early with thy mercy; that we may rejoice and be glad all our days.
[15] Make us glad according to the days wherein thou hast afflicted us, and the years wherein we have seen evil.
[16] Let thy work appear unto thy servants, and thy glory unto their children.
[17] And let the beauty of the LORD our God be upon us: and establish thou the work of our hands upon us; yea, the work of our hands establish thou it.   [King James version]

For the elder Dufour and his children, the opening verse would have intimated that neither Switzerland nor the U.S. was their true home. Thus, their sensation of being dispersed or separated from one another was ultimately illusory. The second, with its evocation of a mountainous landscape, might well have resonated with the Swiss who could, more easily than some, perceive the magnitude and antiquity of creation. The third verse may have reminded them of the unending and senseless cycles of violence that had sundered Christendom and given rise to the very conditions they wished to escape. Next are several lines that speak to the transitory nature of human existence and the brevity of our lives: the implication being that we must reset our perspective to another scale altogether, wherein our daily concerns and decisions -such as a passage to America– are less momentous than they may at first seem. And finally, the very last words of the psalm would have provided an apt benediction and charge for these pietist vine growers: that the work of their hands, cultivating the earth, would conform to God's divine purpose. And with that intention, let us assume, they set forth.

GENERAL REFERENCES

Butler, James L. and John J. Butler. *Indiana Wine: A History*. Indiana University Press, Bloomington and Indianapolis, 2001.

Dufour, John James. *The American Vine-Dresser's Guide*. Editions La Valsainte & Purdue University Press, Vevey [Suisse] and West Lafayette [USA], 2003.

Dufour, Perret. *The Swiss Settlement of Switzerland County, Indiana*. Indianapolis Historical Commission, Indianapolis, 1925.

History of Dearborn, Ohio, and Switzerland Counties from Their Earliest Settlement, vol. 2. Weakley, Harraman & Co., Chicago, 1885.

Knox, Julie LeClerc. *The Dufour Saga, 1796-1942; The Story of the Eight Dufours Who Came from Switzerland and Founded Vevay, Switzerland County, Indiana*. Howell-Goodwin Printing Company, Crawfordsville, Ind., 1942.

Pinney, Thomas. *A History of Wine in America, Volume 1: From the Beginnings to Prohibition*. University of California Press, Berkeley, Los Angeles, and London, 1989.

Verdiel, Auguste. *Histoire du Canton de Vaud*. Martignier et Comp^{e}., Lausanne, 1849-1852 (comprising five volumes).

NOTES

(1) Dufour, John James. *The American Vine-Dresser's Guide*. Editions La Valsainte & Purdue University Press, Vevey [Suisse] and West Lafayette [USA], 2003, p. 32.

(2) "To Thomas Jefferson from John James Dufour, 1 February 1801," *Founders Online,* National Archives, last modified June 13, 2018.
https://founders.archives.gov/?q=Dufour&s=1111311111&r=4
Retrieved November 1, 2018.
[Original source: *The Papers of Thomas Jefferson*, vol. 32, 1 June 1800–16 February 1801, ed. Barbara B. Oberg. Princeton University Press, Princeton, 2005, pp. 529–533.]

(3) "To Thomas Jefferson from John James Dufour, 15 January 1802," *Founders Online,* National Archives, last modified June 13, 2018.
https://founders.archives.gov/?q=Dufour&s=1111311111&r=5
Retrieved November 1, 2018.
[Original source: *The Papers of Thomas Jefferson*, vol. 36, 1 December 1801–3 March 1802, ed. Barbara B. Oberg. Princeton University Press, Princeton, 2009, pp. 373–376.]

(4) Daniel Dufour to Albert Gallatin, January 12, 1802, translated by Chris Momenee. The Papers of Albert Gallatin, Library of Congress, Washington, D.C., 1-2. Extract quoted in "Indiana Wine: A History" by James L. and John J. Butler, p. 36.

(5) "An act to empower John James Dufour, and his associates, to purchase certain lands" in *The Debates and Proceedings in the Congress of the United States; Seventh Congress; comprising the period from December 7, 1801 to May 3, 1802.* Gales & Seaton, publishers, Washington, D.C., 1851, Vol. 11, p. 1356.

(6) "A Covenant of Association for the Settlement of the Lands of Switzerland on the Ohio River," January 20, 1803, in Perret Dufour's *The Swiss Settlement of Switzerland County, Indiana.* Indianapolis Historical Commission, Indianapolis, 1925, pp. 19-21. The thirteen portions were allocated to F. L. Siebenthal (two lots, one being held for his son), J. D. Morerod, P. Bettens, the eight Dufour siblings (including Aimé), and to Jean Jaques Dufour's son, Daniel Vincent Dufour.

(7) Dufour, Jean Jaques. "Broillard de Voyage Pour Jean Jaques Dufour de Sales à Montreux, au Baillage de Vevey" in Perret Dufour's *The Swiss Settlement of Switzerland County, Indiana.* Indianapolis Historical Commission, Indianapolis, 1925, p. 307.)

(Called a "daybook," the "Broillard de Voyage" is not a journal, but a series of memoranda recorded by Dufour covering certain dates between March 20, 1796 – August 20, 1806; and February 20, 1816 – June 23, 1816. The memoranda are almost entirely a record of expenses, purchases and sales, although a few non-pecuniary details do surface. The original is in the collection of the Indiana State Library.)

(8) Butler, James L. and John J. Butler. *Indiana Wine: A History.* Indiana University Press, Bloomington and Indianapolis, 2001, p. 37.

(9) McCoy, John W. "Surname Index" in *The Swiss Settlement of Vevay, Indiana: The Settlers, Their Relatives, Their Associates*, 2014.
http://www.realmac.info/~chevaud/vevay/
Retrieved November 6, 2018.

(10) Dufour, Jean Jaques. "Broillard de Voyage Pour Jean Jaques Dufour de Sales à Montreux, au Baillage de Vevey" in Perret Dufour's *The Swiss Settlement of Switzerland County, Indiana*. Indianapolis Historical Commission, Indianapolis, 1925, p. 285 under July 19, 1798.

(11) Cook, Michael L. and Bettie A. Cook. *Kentucky Court of Appeals Deed Books A-G, vol. 1*. Cook Publications, Evansville, Indiana, 1985, pp. 219-221.

(12) Daniel Dufour's account of the colonists' Atlantic crossing in Julie LeClerc Knox's *The Dufour Saga, 1796-1942: The Story of the Eight Dufours Who Came From Switzerland and Founded Vevay, Switzerland County, Indiana*. Howell-Goodwin Printing Co., Crawfordsville, Indiana, 1942, pp. 20-25.

(13) Dufour, Jean Jaques. "Broillard de Voyage Pour Jean Jaques Dufour de Sales à Montreux, au Baillage de Vevey" in Perret Dufour's *The Swiss Settlement of Switzerland County, Indiana*. Indianapolis Historical Commission, Indianapolis, 1925, pp. 249, 269, 271.

(14) Dufour, Jean Jaques. Letter "To the Citizens of Kentucky," *Kentucky Gazette*, January 17, 1798, p. 2, col. 2-4.

(15) Dufour, Jean Jaques. "To the Honorable the Senate and the House of Representatives of the United States of America," petition dated February 1, 1801, The Thomas Jefferson Papers at the Library of Congress, Manuscript Division.
https://www.loc.gov/manuscripts/?fa=segmentof:mtj1.022_0917_0920/&q=Dufour+1801&st=gallery
Retrieved November 1, 2018.

(16) Alexandre Dubé, Department of History, Washington University, St. Louis. personal communication.

(17) Frey, Donald E. *America's Economic Moralists: A History of Rival Ethics and Economics*. State University of New York Press, Albany, 2009, pp. 63-64.

(18) Engel, Katherine Carté. *Religion and Profit: Moravians in Early America*, University of Pennsylvania Press, Philadelphia, 2009, pp. 32-38.

(19) Sessler, John Jacob. Communal Pietism among Early American Moravians. Henry Holt and Company, New York, 1933, pp. 229-232.

(20) "1762 Brotherly Agreement," translated by Otto Dreydoppel, Jr., Bethlehem Digital History Project, 2002.
http://bdhp.moravian.edu/community_records/regulations/brotherly_agreement/batranslation.html
Retrieved November 1, 2018.

(21) Dufour, Jean Jaques. "Broillard de Voyage Pour Jean Jaques Dufour de Sales à Montreux, au Baillage de Vevey" in Perret Dufour's *The Swiss Settlement of Switzerland County, Indiana*. Indianapolis Historical Commission, Indianapolis, 1925, pp. 303, 307.

(22) Butler, James L. and John J. Butler. *Indiana Wine: A History*. Indiana University Press, Bloomington and Indianapolis, 2001, p. 47.

(23) Dufour, Perret. *The Swiss Settlement of Switzerland County, Indiana*. Indianapolis Historical Commission, Indianapolis, 1925, pp. 63, 68-69.

(24) Butler, James L. and John J. Butler. *Indiana Wine: A History*. Indiana University Press, Bloomington and Indianapolis, 2001, pp. 11,15.

(25) "Census of Population and Housing," United States Bureau of the Census, https://www2.census.gov/prod2/decennial/documents/36894832v2ch06.pdf
Retrieved October 21, 2018.

(26) Dufour, Jean Jaques. "Broillard de Voyage Pour Jean Jaques Dufour de Sales à Montreux, au Baillage de Vevey" in Perret Dufour's *The Swiss Settlement of Switzerland County, Indiana*. Indianapolis Historical Commission, Indianapolis, 1925, p. 285.

(27) Dufour, Jean Jaques. Letter "To the Directors of the Vine Yard Society in Kentucky," *Kentucky Gazette*, July 3, 1800, p. 2, col. 2-3.

(28) Butler, James L. and John J. Butler. *Indiana Wine: A History*. Indiana University Press, Bloomington and Indianapolis, 2001, p. 35.

(29) Dufour, John James to Albert Gallatin, February 1, 1801, trans. Chris Momenee. The Papers of Albert Gallatin, Library of Congress, Washington, D.C., 2. Extract quoted in "Indiana Wine: A History" by James L. and John J. Butler, pp. 27-28.

(30) Dufour, Perret. *The Swiss Settlement of Switzerland County, Indiana*. Indianapolis Historical Commission, Indianapolis, 1925, p. 229.

(31) Sanders, Lewis. "J. J. Dufour – First Vineyard Society of Kentucky –Settlement of Vevay, Indiana" in *Transactions of the Indiana Horticultural Society*, 1872, R. J. Bright, State Printer, Indianapolis, p. 128.

(32) Verdiel, Auguste. *Histoire du Canton de Vaud*. Martignier et Comp^e., Lausanne, 1849-1852, Livre Quatrième (Chapitre XXI) – Livre Cinquième (Chapitres I-III).

(33) Dufour, Jean Jaques. "To the Directors of the Vine Yard Society in Kentucky," *Kentucky Gazette*, July 3, 1800, p. 2, col. 2-3.

(34) "Ordre au Citoyen" no. 281, Le Ministre de La Guerre de la Republique Helvetique Une et Indivisible, Lucerne, April 10, 1799. Document privately owned by Christy Williams, Dallas, Texas.

(35) "Arrête: 1) Le Citoyen Dufour Agent National à Montreux," Le Directoire Exécutif de la Republique Helvetique Une et Indivisible, Lucerne, April 10, 1799.
Document privately owned by Christy Williams, Dallas, Texas.

(36) "From the Revolution to the 19th Century," Ville de Lausanne, http://www.lausanne.ch/en/lausanne-en-bref/lausanne-un-portrait/un-portrait/histoire/revolution-au-xixe-siecle.html
Retrieved November 11, 2018.

(37) Knox, Julie LeClerc. *The Dufour Saga, 1796-1942; The Story of the Eight Dufours Who Came From Switzerland and Founded Vevay, Switzerland County, Indiana*. Howell-Goodwin Printing Co., Crawfordsville, Indiana, 1942, p. 70.

(38) Golay, Humbert. "From the Banks of the Orbe to those of the Ohio: Contribution to the History of the Swiss Colonization in America in 1801" in Ruby Stoner Golay's *David Golay: His Ancestors and Descendants*, Des Moines, Iowa, 1984, pp. 7-12.

(39) Knox, Julie LeClerc. *The Dufour Saga, 1796-1942; The Story of the Eight Dufours Who Came From Switzerland and Founded Vevay, Switzerland County, Indiana*. Howell-Goodwin Printing Co., Crawfordsville, Indiana, 1942, p. 34.

(40) Dufour, Jean Jaques. "Letter of a Vine-dresser to his Children" in *The Panoplist and Missionary Magazine*, Boston, 1817, Vol. 13, no. 6, pp. 248-255.

(41) Dufour, Jean Jaques. "Letter from a Father in Switzerland to his Children in America" in *The Panoplist and Missionary Magazine*, Boston, 1817, Vol. 13, no. 8, pp. 348-352.

(42) "The Abbots," La Confriére des Vignerons de Vevey, https://www.confreriedesvignerons.ch/en/presentation/the-abbots/ Retrieved November 8, 2018.

(43) Knox, Julie LeClerc. *The Dufour Saga, 1796-1942; The Story of the Eight Dufours Who Came From Switzerland and Founded Vevay, Switzerland County, Indiana*. Howell-Goodwin Printing Co., Crawfordsville, Indiana, 1942, p. 19.

(44) Butler, James L. and John J. Butler. *Indiana Wine: A History*. Indiana University Press, Bloomington and Indianapolis, 2001, p. 32.

Appendix 1

Transcriptions of the 1800 Compact/1800 Lettre were prepared by Anna Auger Tonkin and Anne Hajek, from which the following line-by-line version was developed in 2018. Brackets containing ellipses [... ...] indicate illegible script or areas of paper loss in the manuscript. Words or letters within brackets are inferences. While every attempt has been made to accurately replicate spelling and punctuation, the original should always be consulted in order to obtain a precise quotation.

Les Sous Signés Parens & Amis ont formé le Pacte Suivant.

Considérant que [c'est dans] l'ordre de la nature, que des Pères & mères portent leurs premiers soins à [élever] leurs Enfans dans la [crainte de] Dieu, en leur donnant une éducation de la quelle ils puissent tirer les [concepts de] morale & de justice qui [caractérisent/marquent] le vrai Chrétiens, & de pourvoir en même tems a leur bien être [temporel] en cherchant a leur procurer un établissement convenable à l'homme de bien, qui, en travaillant à la culture des [terres] remplit le but du Créateur, évite les pièges que les arts, l'industrie & le commerce en Europe tendent sans cesse a [la] vertu & a la moralité de ceux qui s'y adonnent.

Considérant, que les bouleverssemens & les guerres qui desolent l'Europe, semblent être l'Effet de la trop gr[ande] population, qui occasionne un choc continuel pour le terme de propriéte, & tend a renverser les notions de [Justice] qui font la base du bonheur social.

Considérant, que les idées que nous nous sommes formés des principes socieaux, la liberté & l'Egalité, se trou[vent] dans la constitution des Etats Unis d'Amérique & puissamment soutenue par la moralité des Peuples Americains.

Considérant, que pour remplir les vües de la bonne Providence, l'imence & fertile continent du nouveau monde [va] être peuplé & cultivé, & que ceux qui ont la Sagesse & le courage de quitter les frivoles & dangereuses [... ...] actuellement en Suisse, seront protégés par elle & combles de ses bénédictions.

Considérant enfin, que cette bonne Providence à déja signalé sa puissante protection en faveur de nôtre cher [et] digne ami Jean Jaques Dufour, qui depuis quatre ans, travaille avec succès a la culture de la vigne en Amérique & à procurer nôtre futur établissement, ou l'alliance intime que nous formons ensembles ; (que par conséquent, nous devons accélerer autant qu'il est en nôtre pouvoir l'éxécution de cette entreprise) en multipliant les ressources, en travaillant & aquerant des terres necessaires a la collonie & C^a Convenons & arrètons :

Titre 1. Du départ, de l'ordre du Voyage & des fraix de transport.

Article 1. Chaque Chef de famille fournira a la dépense de sa famille en proportion du nombre & des Equipages qui lui [sont] necessaire, le tout calculé sur des bases équitables ; le départ est fixé dans la première quinzaine de Novembre prochain.

Art : 2. Ne sont point compris dans les Equipages particuliers, les objets qui seront destinés à l'établissement de la Commun[auté] tels que les Plantons d'Arbres fruitiers, Chapons de Vigne, Graines de Diversses plantes d'Europe, Outils & généralement tout q[ue] sera destiné à être mis en comunion, tous ces objets devant être aquis & transportés à fraix communs.

Art : 3. Il est de même entendu que les Chars & Chevaux pour la route jusqu'à l'endroit de l'embarquement, seront fournis à fraix communs, & les pertes qui pourroient résulter en les vendant au port seront [...] portés par tous les membres de la société, en raison de la part nécessaire qu'ils y auront.

Art : 4. Il sera nommé deux membres de la Société, qui seront spécialement chargés de l'économie du Voyage, du [soutenir et] de pourvoir a la sureté des Equipages, de tenir les Comptes de dépense & de S'enquerir exactement de l'Etat & de la Santé de[s] Voyageurs, afin de leur procurer le régime convenable ; ils pourront se diviser entreux cette intendance de manière que chaque partie en soit exactement soignée.

Art : 5. Les Mères de famille soigneront les petits Enfans, & les Jeunes filles les Secouderont de tout leur pouvoir ; les jeunes Garçons en état de soigner quelques parties dans la conduite du voyage, seront aux ordres des deux Intendants qui leur assigneront ce qu'ils auront à faire.

Art : 6. Dès que l'embarquement sera arrêté avec le Capitaine du Veusseau, il sera pourvu à l'emplette des petites provisions qui peuvent contribuer au bien être des femmes & des Enfans pendant le cours de la traversée ; il sera fait (s'il y a lieu) une convention avec le Capitaine, pour que les malades le cas arrivant puissent être logés dans la cabine ; les deux Intendants du Voyage veilleront à ce que le Sèxe soit respecté & que rien ne puisse compromettre les règles de la décence & de la moralité.

Titre 2. Religion, Education.

Art : 7. La Réligion que nous professons sera maintenue & transmise à nos Enfans, elle repose sur la stricte observation de la morale Évangelique, qui servira de base a l'éducation de la Jeunesse. Le Culte que nous estimons être le plus agreable à Dieu, est la pratique de toutes les vertus sociales ; mais pour nourrir & fortifier ces dispositions, le jour du Dimanche sera consacré à lui rendre nos homages, à le remercier de ses bienfaits en implorant Sa bénédiction.

Art : 8. Jusques-à-ce-que nous soyons a portée d'avoir un Ministre de la Religion, consacré Selon l'usage de l'Eglise

Chrétienne, il sera choisi parmis nous un Régent de la Collonie dont les fonctions seront :
- a. De faire la prière les jours de Fêtes & Dimanches.
- b. De soigner l'instruction de la Jeunesse dans la morale Chrétienne, de lui enseigner l'Ecriture, l'ortographe & l'arrithmétique.
- c. Il -résidera le tribunal de famille & surveillera la conservation des bonnes moeurs.

Art : 9. Les fonctions du Régent ne le dispenseront point du travail de l'agriculture, ce sera dans la Saison morte qu'il donnera des leçons, & cette occupation alors lui tiendra lieu d'autres travaux qui se font pendant l'hivers, il ne jouira d'aucune autre distinction que celle que lui méritera la régularité de sa Conduite & son Zêle à remplir les dévo[irs] importants qui lui sont confiés.

Titre 3.   Aquisitions, travail, Propriétés comunes & particuliéres.

Art : 10. Il ne pourra y avoir aucune division de propriété avant l'espace de <u>Dix Ans révolus</u> d'une enti[ère]

comm[union]

_____*fin de la page 1, version originale*_____

[communion... ... ...] terres aquises que de leur culture & production [... ... ...]
[... ... ..t] pour faire règner l'équité & l'émulation, il sera règlé [ci après d... ...]elle manière chaque
[Chef] de fam[ille pourra] retirer par la Suitte le juste équivalant de ce que lui app[artien]dra, proportionnellement a sa
[...] de fonds pour les achats de terrin, aux bras qu'il aura fourni pour la [... ...] aux Enfants ou autres Personnes
que la Société aura nouri & ellevés, les quels n'auront pas travailler pour leur [...]retient.

Art : 12ᵉ. Comme les mises de fonds pour l'achat des terres ne sont pas proprement la principale richesse
de la Société en comparaison de leur défrichement & des moyens d'en faire Valoir les productions ; ces
mises seront compencées par l'interet à tant pour % qui sera payé a chacun, ou porté en compte,
de l'entier de sa mise & sera évalué après que la valeur des fonds sera exactement connue.

Art : 13ᵉ. Au bout de chaque année il sera fait une apréciation générale du travail qu'aura fourni
chaque Chef de famille ou Associé, tant par lui-même que par ses Enfans en état de travailler, que par
les ouvrièrs qu'il aurait eu le moyen de fournir sous déductions de la consomation faite par les individus
[de] sa famille hors d'Etat de travailler.

Art : 14ᵉ. D'après cette base, il sera ouvert à chaque Chef un compte particulier ou il sera spécifié la
[p]ortion qu'il a à l'établissement, ce qui sera déterminé par fraction, comme par Exemple : s'il a
fourni un Dixième du travail, le fond défriché lui appartiendra la dixième partie pʳ· l'année calculée.

Art : 15ᵉ. Et comme il pourra y avoir de la variation, c'est-à-dire que toutes les années ne seront pas égales,
ces comptes particuliers seront ouverts pendant <u>Dix ans,</u> au bout des quels il sera détermine quelle
sera la portion de chaque famille dans l'établissement.

Art : 16ᵉ. Pour que la valeur des productions suive la même proportion, le produit sera entièrement
employé à l'avancement de la culture des terres communes, a procurer & payer les Ouvriers qui seront
entretenu par la Société.

Art : 17ᵉ. Notre Ami Jean Jaques Dufour, sous les auspices du quel le présent Contract doit avoir son entière
exécution, sera prie par plusieurs lettres qui lui seront adressées incessamment, de faire l'aquisition des terres
necessaires a la confection du plan de la Société, tant pour la culture de la vigne que pour les autres cultures
qui pourroient être entreprises & cela à titre d'avance de même que de procurer les vivres nécéssaires
jusques-à-ce-qu'on puisse les recolter sur les terres de la Sociéte, bien entendu que par une juste
évaluation il aura une p[... ...]rte portion dans l'Etablissement suivant les dispositif des Arts 12. 13. 14. 15. 16. du présent titre.

Art : 18ᵉ. Il sera invité a [...] courier le présent Contract & même à indiquer les changemens qui [lui sont] convenables.

Art : 19ᵉ. Mais dans aucun cas il ne pourra Changer le principe fondamantal de comunion avec sa famille
ni proposer aux Associés de ne les recevoir que comme Ouvriers [...] ou les abandonner seuls en les separant
de sa famille : c'est de quoi son frère Daniel Dufour rép[ond], s'engageant formellement que sous les

reserves & compansations stipulées dans les Articles précédents, la complette indivision pendant Dix ans
ne pourra point être Altérèe.

Titre 4ᵉ.   Batimens, Habillemens, Nourriture.

Art : 20ᵉ. Jusques-à-ce-que les facultés de la Société soyent accruent au de la du simple nécessaire, il ne sera
entrepris aucune Bâtisse que celles indispensables aux logemens Rustiques de la Collonie.

Art : 21ᵉ. Les Habillemens seront simples & modestes, mais proprement entretenus, la malpropreté devant
être interdite, au surplus chacun s'habillera à ses fraix.

Art : 22ᵉ. La nourriture sera la même pour tous, la frugalité, la simplicité, l'économie & la plus
grande propreté doivent constituer le régime de la Société.

Titre 5ᵉ.   Fêtes & Divertissements.

[Art : 23ᵉ.] Il y aura outre les Dimanches & Fêtes ordinaires, quatre grandes solemnités chaque année savoir :
—L'Anniversaire du jour ou Jean Jaques Dufour débarqua en Amérique ; —Celui du jour ou il planta
la prémière Vigne. —Celui du jour de nôtre débarquement en Amérique ; —Enfin celui du jour
ou nous embrasserons pour la première fois dans le Nouveau Monde nôtre Précurceur Jⁿ. Jaqs. Dufour.
Les Divertissements seront toujours précédés de Prières & d'actions de graces à l'<u>Etre Supreme</u> par le
Régent, qui ensuite dirigera la Fête d'une manière analogue aux circonstances ou nous nous
trouverons. L'ordre & la décence seront partout scrupuleusement observé.

Titre 6ᵉ.   Tribunal de Famille.

Art : 24. Il est entendu entre nous que nous nous soumettons entièrement aux Lois du Pais que nous
allons habiter, & nous prions le Très Haut de nous confirmer par une heureuse expérience dans la
persuasion ou nous sommes que jamais le crime ou les querelles ne souilleront nôtre Société, & que
les Lois ne seront jamais que protectrices envers nous.

Art : 25ᵉ. Pour terminer les petits differens qui pourroient s'élever entre les membres de la Société, pour

faire

_____*fin de la page 2, version originale*_____

faire respecter la décence & maintenir une Stricte Moralité de mêm[e que] pour reprime[r la]
paresse & les négligences, il y aura un Tribunal de famille composé des quatre plus Anciens [de la]
Société & Présidé par le Régent, outre deux autres membres de la Société que le Prévenu a ca
droit de choisir s'il le trouve à propos & par ce moyen augmenter de deux membres le nombre des Juges.

Art : 26ᵉ. Le Tribunal de famille prononcera arbitralement sur tous les cas mentionnés dans l'article précédent.
Il pourra infliger des Peines & des humiliations, telles que d'assigner au coupable un certin genre de travail,
une place séparée pour manger & des mets differents infèrieurs à ceux des repas ordinaires, la privation des
divertissemens pour un tems limité & même des amandes pécuniaires, qui seront destinées à acheter des Livres
utiles aux Jeunes Gens, du Papier & des plumes, ces Amandes entreront dans les comptes de famille.

Art : 27ᵉ. Ceux au contraire qui se distingueront par leur amour pour le travail, l'activité, l'assiduité & sur tout par une
conduite exemplaire, recevront des encouragemens & des marques de bienveuillance de la part de la Société,
tels que les prémière place â table, des places de distinctions dans les divertissemens, des couronne d'honneur,
des Bouquets le Dimanche, outre cela il leur sera fait présent de quelque habillemens qui porteront les
jours de Fêtes.

Titre 7ᵉ.   Evénemens à Prevoir.

Art : 28ᵉ. Il est convenu qu'en cas de mort soit en route soit dans la Collonie d'un Chef de famille ou de son représentant, la Veuve & les Orphelins ne pourront être privés d'aucun des avantages de la Société, laquelle les adopte & représentent en tous lieux & occasions le Chef décédér les recevant & admettant à tous égard en son lieu & place.

Art : 29ᵉ. Il est possible qu'étant une fois sur les lieux de l'établissement projetté, il conviendra d'apporter quelques changemens aux présénts règlemens, d'y ajouter de nouveaux articles, ce qui pourra avoir lieu sur la proposition d'un membre de la Société, lors que les deux tiers plus un y donneront leur consentement, mais dans aucun cas on ne pourra mettre en déliberation de changer le principe de communion pendant Dix ans, n'y déroger en aucune manière au contenu de l'article vingt-huit.

Art : 30ᵉ. Les tiers mentionnés dans le précédent article seront comptés dans l'ordre suivant : Le tiers de cinc sera deux, le tiers de huit sera trois, le tiers de onze sera quatre & ainsi de suitte ; ce calcul aura lieu [toutes] les fois que le nombre des votans ne poura donner deux tiers justes.

Art : 31ᵉ. Toute les fois qu'il surviendra des changemens a faire, ou qui sera fait des propositions qui éxigeron[t] d'être mis en déliberation ; l'objet sera décidé par un conseil général des Chefs de famille soit contracté dans le quel seront admis les Mères de famille [& les Garçons ayant atteint l'age] de Vingt ans, ils [… …]

Le présent contract en trente-un articles sera réligieusement observé par les contractés [...] nous en donnons pour garantie l'affirmation libre & sincère au nom de l'Être Suprême, duquel n[ous] implorons la bénédiction, & engageons la généralité de nos biens présents & futur. Ainsi fait & passé au Chenit District de la Vallée du Lac de Joux, Canton du Leman en Suisse, le trentiéme Avril Mille huit Cent—le 30ᵉ Avril 1800.

Signé à l'Original   tous au nom de leur famille respective

        Dˡ Dufour de Montreux
        David Golay de la Vallée du Lac de Joux
        Philippe Berney   "   "   "
        Joseph Meylan   "   "   "
        Jⁿ Pʳʳᵉ Daniel Borralley de Blonay   Maître Charpentier
_____

à Sales de Montreux—Du 26 Juin 1800.

      Le 14ᵉ. Mars dernier mon bien aimé frère & cher Ami ! J'ai remis une lettre pour toi aux citoyens Genand de Vevey, fils du Tourneur accompagné de son ami Trottet (fils de celui qui tient les bains de [derrière] l'Aile), lesquels sont partit, le jour suivant pour se rendre à Bourdeaux & de la s'embarquer pʳ l'Amérique, mais je viens d'apprendre par leurs Pres qu'ils ne se sont pas embarqués, ayant trouvé les tems trop dangereux & sur tout le prix d'embarquement trop cher, ils ont passés en Espagne, renvoyant la partie jusqu'à-ce que l'occasion soit plus favorable, de sorte que je ne sai pas s'ils auront fait partir ma lettre, dans l'incertitude ou je suis à cet égard je vai t'en repetter quelques phrases dans celle-ci. —Dès lors j'ai reçu ta bien agréable lettre de Firstvineyard proche de Léxinton dans le Kentuky du 15 Xᵗʳ 1799 plus une petite lettre incluse dans une de M. Mennet a son pére à Lausanne même datte ; dans la prémière je vois que tu te félicitois ainsi que toute la famille de pouvoir nous embrasser ce printemps ; mais hélas ! nos esperances ont été deçuës encore cette fois ; cependant tout s'ameillore, les choses Politiques paroissent prendre de jour en jour une tournure plus favorable a la paix, & j'espère que dans le cours de Janvier ou février de 1801. Toute la famille (accompagnée des Amis & amies qui doivent Dieu Aidant former la collonie dont le Pacte est au commencement [de] cette lettre) auront le doux plaisir de t'embrasser. ô mon cher frère ! que cette esperance remplis nos co[eurs] de joye ; Tous nos voeux s'adressent à l'Être Suprême pour qu'il daigne dans la miséricorde infinie, [benir]

_____*fin de la page 3, version originale*_____

[nôtre] entreprïse [afin qu'elle] prospere. Nous te prions en même tems d'employer tous tes moyens pour nous [aider.]
   Les Signataires [ou Chefs de] l'Association désireorient d'établir la collonie sur les Bords Nórd Ouest de l'Ohio […] le milleux de son cours, croyant cet emplacement le plus convenable & le meilleur tant pour la fertili[té] du terrin que pʳ la Salubrité de l'aire, du moins suivant ce qu'en disent qqles Auteurs que nous avons lu, & sur tout ta lettre écritte de Newyork du 23ᵉ Juillet 1798.—Nous réunissons en Société a peu près tout

ce qu'il faut pour former un établissement complet ; nous avons Maitre marechal, M^tre Charpantier [...]
pour la construction des Bâtimens que p^r. celle des Pressoirs, Moulin à Sie & autres ouvrages de [charpenterie]
et Ménuiserie, Maitre fruitier, soit Vacher, Tailleur & Tisserand, il ne nous manque qu'un Tanneur & un
Cordonnier, mais il n'est pas dit que nous ne puissions réunir tout cela par la suitte.—Je te prie donc
au nom de toute la Société, de tâcher de nous acheter les terres nécessaires a la confection de nos plans
et de les choisir aussi bien que possible, nous en laissons le choix a ta prudence ; quand a la quantité,
elle ne doit guère être moindre de 4 à 5 mille acres, car nous serons une grande collonie ; ce qui [t'empêche]
[peut] être le plus c'est de savoir ou prendre p^r les payer, il te faut tâcher de les avoir a crédit au moins jus[qu'à]
[nôtre] arrivée, nous ferons de sorte d'apporter les fonds nécessaires pour cela.—J'aime aussi croire que [tu]
approuvera ce plan de nôtre assiation ; du moins je l'ai signé dans cette espérance, il plait à toute la
famille, principalement à nôtre Père, malgré hélas qu'il ne pourra pas en profiter avec nous a cause de
ses infirmités, il restera pour tenir compagnie à ta femme, que tes soins, tes promessses, ton Amour &
tout-ce qu'ont pu lui dire les Gens de bien qui pensent comme nous, ne peuvent [changer ses caprices...] la décider à quitter un
pais, ou les riens qui l'attache, ont plus d'empire sur son coeur que tous les sublimes Sentiments que tu as
pour elle & le bonheur de son fils, du quel je suis fort content car il promet beaucoup, il ne lui manque
pour en faire un homme, qu'un Maitre tel que toi, afin de soigner son Education ; il en possede déja les prémiers
éllémens, il écrit passablement bien pour son age, lit encore mieux, même l'écrit de main ; son coeur est
sur tout exellent, capable de recevoir le germe ou le principe de toutes les vertus Chrétiennes & sociales
se les rendre un jour avec energie ; cependant la Mère ne néglige pas son éducation, elle l'envoye
régulliérement aux ecoles eté & hivers, [...] il va maintenant à celle de Chernex comme nous y aillons
autre fois c'est-à-dire il monte le matin & redesant le soir.

Je reviens à nôtre plan d'association ; Ce qui m'a fait à y Souscrire est fondé sur deux raisons, la première
[la principale le selon nous consiste] dans la bonheur de pouvoir vivre avec de vrais Amis ; dont les Vértus
[... ... ...]
ou bien être de la choisir aussi bonne qui lui est possible de la trouver sur tout lors qu'il en a la faculté.
La Seconde est une raison d'interet ou d'économie qui coincide avec facultés pécuniaires & Plus que [...]
tu sentira aussi bien que moi l'avantage qu'il y a de former une Société telle que la nôtre pour entreprendre
le défrichement d'un grand terrin ; nous aurions été faibles de nôtre propre faiblesse, au lieu que nous seront
fort de la force & des moyens de tous, tant pour la construction des Batimens que pour celle des artifices & autres objets de première
nécessite ; voila mon cher frère en Abrégé les considérations qui m'ont engagé à signer ce plan d'Association ;
cependant, aprésent que je l'ai un peu mieux examiné, j'y trouve un grand changement à faire & qques articles
à y ajouter : Dabord ; le terme de dix années sans pouvoir Rompre ou diviser la Société me parait trop
Long, c'est se lier les bras à tous ; Boralley est du même avis, ainsi je vais écrire a la Vallée pour
inviter les Amis Signataires de là a consentir que le terme soit réduit à six années au lieu de Dix.
Tu peux donc compter la dessus. Quand nous aurons fait une épreuve de 4 à 5 années sur les lieux
si nous voyons que le terme de six années soit trop court pour le bien de nos interets, nous serons
toujours libre de l'augmenter. Quant aux articles à ajouter, cela poura se faire sur les lieux.
Tu verra par ce plan que nôtre départ est fixé dans la prémière 15^en de Novembre prochain,
si la guerre ou autres événemens imprévus n'y apportent obstacle ; nous ne négligerons rien de nôtre
côté pour en accélerer les préparatifs, si seulement le ciel accorde à nos voeux que la paix se fasse d'ici
alors, & que nous puissions passer par la France, car si nous étions obligés de passer par
Hambourg, nos moyens pecuniaires ne seroient peut-être suffisants pour faire ce grand tour
et probablement impraticable dans cette saison arrive des glaces, cependant c'est au mois de
Novembre que nous devons partir pour pouvoir prendre avec nous une pacotille de chapo[ns de]
Vigne & des Arbres fruitiers dont nous serons sufisamment fourni de differantes espèces & qualité.
Depuis le départ de ma lettre du 14e Mars dernier, il s'est bien passé des choses extraordinaires, d[ont]
sans doute les papiers nouvelles vous instruiront. L'Immortel Buonaparte à conduit dans 25 jours
dans le cours du mois passé une Armée forte d'environ 70 Mille hommes de Paris à Millan à
travers le Pais de Vaud, le bas Vallais & le grand S^t. Bernard ; tu peux juger par là combien de troupes
nous avons eu à loger. Le 13 May, le marché de Vevey à été plus brillant que jamais on ne l'aye vu depuis que
[...iste] ; Buonaparte en personne accompagné de Six ou Sept autre Generaux français ya passé en revué trois

[demi]

_____*la lettre s'arrête ici*_____

Appendix 2

In preparing this report, I found it useful to develop a chronologic list of the principal documents concerning Jean Jaques Dufour (1763-1827). The table beginning on page 58 presents this information and is offered with the hope that someone else may find it moderately helpful. Note, however, that it is an incomplete list; for example, Switzerland County court records and deeds have not been included.

Abbreviations used in the table are:

ACV = Archives Contonales Vaudoises, Rue de la Mouline 32, 1022 Chavannes-près-Renens, Suisse.

APSL = American Philosophical Society Library, 105 S. 5th St, Philadelphia, Pennsylvania, 19106.

AVG (1826) = *The American Vine-Dresser's Guide*, by John James Dufour. S. J. Browne (publisher), Cincinnati, 1826. Original edition.

AVG (2003) = *The American Vine-Dresser's Guide*, by John James Dufour. La Valsainte & Purdue University Press, Vevey, Suisse and West Lafayette, Indiana, 2003. Rewritten in modern English by Carol Louise Hartman; with a foreword by Christian Blickenstorfer, and commentaries by Yves Bordet, Bruce Bordelon, James L. Butler, and John J. Butler.

CHLA = Cincinnati History Library and Archives, 1301 Western Avenue, Cincinnati, Ohio, 45203.

CW = Christy Williams, descendent of Antoinette Dufour (1781-1857), and owner of six documents received from the collection of Julie LeClerc Knox.

DP = *The Debates and Proceedings in the Congress of the United States; Seventh Congress; comprising the period from December 7, 1801 to May 3, 1802*. Gales & Seaton, publishers, Washington, D.C., 1851.

HDOS = *History of Dearborn, Ohio, and Switzerland Counties, Indiana from their Earliest Settlement*. Weakley, Harraman & Co., Chicago, 1885.

IHS = Indiana Historical Society, 450 W. Ohio Street, Indianapolis, Indiana, 46202.

ISL = Indiana State Library, 315 W. Ohio St., Indianapolis, Indiana, 46202.

IW = *Indiana Wine: A History*, by James L. and John J. Butler. Indiana University Press, Bloomington and Indianapolis, 2001.

LC = Library of Congress, 101 Independence Ave. SE, Washington, D.C. 20540

PMM = *The Panoplist and Missionary Magazine*, published from 1808 to 1817 by Jedediah Morse in Boston, Massachusetts.

PTJ = *The Papers of Thomas Jefferson*, Princeton University Press, (various editors).

SSSC = *The Swiss Settlement of Switzerland County, Indiana*, by Perret Dufour. Indiana Historical Commission, Indianapolis, 1925.

TDS = *The Dufour Saga, 1796-1942*, by Julie LeClerc Knox. Howell-Goodwin Printing Company, Crawfordsville, Ind., 1942.

TP = *Territorial Papers of the United States*, compiled and translated by Clarence Edwin Carter. U.S. Printing Office, Washington, D.C., 1939.

UV = University of Virginia, Alderman Library, 160 McCormick Rd, Charlottesville, Virginia.

USSL = *U.S. Statutes at Large*, Government Printing Office, Washington, D.C., 1813. Vol. 6, p. 126.

Guide to Dufour-related documents, 1762 – 1826

Document date:	Document title, or description:	Location of Original:	Appears in:	Notes:
24 Jun 1762	"Reconnaissance de Communage de Noville and Rennaz"	ISL, Indianapolis	SSSC, pp. 220-223	SSSC provides both a transcription in French and its English translation. Document certifying that the sons of Jean Jaques Rodolph Dufour (1694-1778) hold rights in the communes of Noville and Rennaz.
21 Feb 1763	Baptism record for Jean Jaques Dufour	ACV, Chavannes-pres-Rennens	AVG (2003), p. 15	Record shows that the birth occurred 14 Feb 1763; names his parents; church not indicated. AVG provides only a photograph of the record, and the citation "Archives Cantonales Vaudoises, E/b, p. 65."
Jan 1796	Jean Jaques Dufour's departure certificate for the Americas	ACV, Chavannes-pres-Rennens	AVG (2003), p. 15	AVG provides only a photograph of the record, which is difficult to decipher, and the citation "Archives Cantonales Vaudoises, E/a, 31."
20 Mar 1796 – 23 Jun 1816	"Broillard de Voyage pour Jean Jaques Dufour" (or, "Daybook of John James Dufour")	ISL, Indianapolis	SSSC, pp. 234-347	SSSC provides both a transcription and its English translation.
19 Dec 1796	Letter to George Washington, by Jean Jaques Dufour	UV, Charlottesville		In French, concerning Ohio Valley lands that Washington owned and was then selling. May be viewed online at https://founders.archives.gov/?q=Dufour&s=1111311111&r=3
10 Jan 1798	"Letter to the Citizens of Kentucky" by Jean Jaques Dufour			Published on 17 Jan 1798 in the *Kentucky Gazette* on page 2, columns 2-4. May be viewed online at http://nyx.uky.edu/dips/xt763x83js47/data/1733.pdf

Date	Document	Source	Notes
10 Sep 1798	"Public Notice" by J. Russell on behalf of the Kentucky Association for the Establishment of a Vineyard	IW, p. 18	Published on 19 Sep 1798 in the *Kentucky Gazette* on page 1, column 3. May be viewed online at http://nyx.uky.edu/dips/xt77d7957m7g/data/1906.pdf
10 Apr 1799	Military appointment, Daniel Dufour	CW, Dallas, Texas	Issued by "Le Ministre de la Guerre de la Republique Helvétique."
10 Apr 1799	Military appointment, Daniel Dufour	CW, Dallas, Texas	Issued by "Le Directoire Executif de la Republique Helvétique."
30 Apr 1800	Handwritten copy of a compact drafted and signed by the prospective Swiss colonists (**"1800 Compact"**)	CW, Dallas, Texas	This document includes an appended letter from Daniel Dufour to Jean Jaques Dufour dated 26 Jun 1800 (see below under 26 Jun 1800).
23 Jun 1800	"Letter to the Directors of the Vine Yard Society in Kentucky," by Jean Jaques Dufour		Published on 3 Jul 1800 in the *Kentucky Gazette* on page 2, columns 2-3. May be viewed online at http://nyx.uky.edu/dips/xt7vdn3zt515/data/2832.pdf
26 Jun 1800	Handwritten letter from Daniel Dufour to Jean Jaques Dufour (**"1800 Lettre"**)	CW, Dallas, Texas	This is appended to the 30 April 1800 Compact (see above). The letter is lengthy but is missing its last page(s).
ca. 3 Jul 1800	"Reply to Dufour Letter," by the Kentucky Vineyard Society		Published on 3 Jul 1800 in the *Kentucky Gazette* on page 2, column 2. May be viewed online at http://nyx.uky.edu/dips/xt7vdn3zt515/data/2832.pdf

Date	Document	Location	Source	Notes
5 Aug 1800	Contract between Jean Jaques Dufour and the Kentucky Vineyard Society			Discussed in IW, pp. 20-21. Its authors cite Michael L. and Bettie A. Cook, "Kentucky Court of Appeals Deed Books A-G, vol. 1 (Evansville, Ind.: Cook Publications, 1985, pp. 219-221).
20 Dec 1800	"Acte Civique et d'origine pour le Cit. Daniel Dufour de Montreux"	CW, Dallas, Texas		Document certifying Daniel Dufour as a citizen of the Helvetica Republic.
13 Jan 1801	"Pattente pour Jean Jaques Dufour Fils"	ISL, Indianapolis	SSSC, p. 218-219	SSSC includes a photograph of the original document in French; and then provides an English translation. Grants *in loco parentis* responsibility to Jean Jaques Dufour, Jr.; signed by Jean Jaques Dufour, Sr.
1801	Daniel Dufour's account of the colonists' voyage to America (diary extract?)		TDS, pp. 20-24	In TDS, Julie Knox relied on a translation "found in 1929 among the papers of Josephine Detraz Shadday." The ISL has in its collection a 1917 transcript of an English translation...perhaps the same document used by Knox.
26 Jan 1801	"Grand Festival"			An article published on 26 Jan 1801 in the *Kentucky Gazette* on pages 2-3. Jean Jaques Dufour received a toast. May be viewed online at http://kdl.kyvl.org/catalog/xt7ns17sns24_2?
1 Feb 1801	Letter to Albert Gallatin, by Jean Jaques Dufour	LC, Washington, D.C.		Albert Gallatin Papers. Letter translated by Thomas Harris. Cited in IW, where an extract is quoted on pp. 27-28.

Date	Document	Source	Notes
1 Feb 1801	Letter to Thomas Jefferson, by Jean Jaques Dufour	PTJ, vol. 32, pp. 529-533	Thomas Jefferson Papers. This letter is available online (Founders Online, National Archive) at https://founders.archives.gov/?q=Dufour&s=1111311111&r=4 Includes French transcription, a recent English translation, editorial notes. pdfs of this letter are available at https://picryl.com/topics/jean+jacques+dufour
1 Feb 1801	Petition to Congress, by Jean Jaques Dufour		Thomas Jefferson Papers. This document is available as a pdf online at https://picryl.com/topics/jean+jacques+dufour The petition is in English and was enclosed in the letter to Jefferson.
11 Feb 1801	Letter to Federal Land Office at Cincinnati, by Jean Jaques Dufour (**"1801 Translation/1801 Letter"**)	CHLA, Cincinnati	In this letter, Jean Jaques Dufour enclosed his English translation of the 1800 Compact.
6 Jul 1801	"American Independence!"		Published on 6 July 1801 in the *Kentucky Gazette*, page 2, columns 1-2. A toast was made to the Swiss settlers. May be viewed online at http://nyx.uky.edu/dips/xt7mkk94853t/data/3206.pdf
6 Jul 1801	Notice of arrival of the Swiss settlers		Published on 6 July 1801 in the *Kentucky Gazette*, page 2, column 2. May be viewed online at http://nyx.uky.edu/dips/xt7mkk94853t/data/3206.pdf
Jul 1801	"Letter to the Tennessee Gazette," by Jean Jaques Dufour		Published in the *Tennessee Gazette* on 29 July 1801. Cited in IW, pp. 33-34.
29 Jul 1801	Notice of arrival of the Swiss settlers		Published in the newspaper, "Cincinnati Western Spy." Cited in IW, p. 34.

Date	Document	Location	Reference	Notes
12 Jan 1802	Letter to Albert Gallatin, by Daniel Dufour	LC, Washington, D.C.		Albert Gallatin Papers. Letter translated by Chris Momenee. Extract quoted in IW, p. 36.
15 Jan 1802	Letter to Thomas Jefferson, by Jean Jaques Dufour		PTJ, vol. 36, pp. 373-376	Thomas Jefferson Papers. This letter is available online (Founders Online, National Archive) https://founders.archives.gov/?q=Dufour&s=1111311111&r=5 Includes French transcription, English translation, editorial notes. pdfs of this letter are available at https://picryl.com/topics/jean+jacques+dufour
1 May 1802	"An act to empower John James Dufour, and his associates, to purchase certain lands"		DP, vol. 11, p. 1356	This Congressional act secured four sections of land for the establishment of the Swiss Colony in (what would become) Switzerland County, Indiana. May be viewed online through Google Books ("Annals of the Congress of the United States… Seventh Congress").
12 June 1802	"Cession de la flachere de derriere les murs de Villeneuve"	ISL, Indianapolis		Document wherein Jean Jaques Dufour, Sr. transfers title of a "flachere" to his grandson (Jean Jaques Dufour, Jr.'s son) Daniel Vincent Dufour.
12 Oct 1802	"Notice" by J. J. Dufour re. his intention to patent a kiln			Published on 12 October 1802 in the *Kentucky Gazette*, page 3, column 1. May be viewed online at http://nyx.uky.edu/dips/xt75dv1ck84f/data/3479.pdf
1802 and later	Maps and surveys of the Swiss Colony, its vineyards, etc.	ISL, Indianapolis	see IW, pp. 19 and 29	Includes a survey map of the First Vineyard property in Kentucky.

20 Jan 1803	Handwritten copy of "Convenant d'association pour l'établissement des terres de Suisserland sur le Fleuve de l'Ohio"	CW, Dallas, Texas	(SSSC, pp. 19-21) (HDOS, pp. 993-995)	With this agreement, the Swiss settlers divided the land received through Congress into equal-sized allotments. CW's copy must not be one used by Perret Dufour in SSSC, as his version includes signatures, a seal, and an appended certification. SSSC provides only an English translation.
29 Mar 1803	Untitled article concerning a meeting of the Kentucky Vineyard Society wherein First Vineyard's first vintage was tasted			Published on 29 March 1803 in the *Kentucky Gazette*, page 3, column 1. May be viewed online at http://nyx.uky.edu/dips/xt7np55dcj6s/data/0042.pdf
1 Jan 1804	"Letter from a Vine-dresser to his Children," by Jean Jaques Dufour, Sr.		PMM, vol. 13, no. 6, pp. 248-255	Available online (Google Books). This is a sermon authored by Jean Jaques Dufour, Sr. addressed to his children in America.
7 Feb 1804	Letter to Thomas Jefferson, by Louis Gex-Oboussier		PTJ, vol. 42, pp. 416-418	Thomas Jefferson Papers. This letter is available online (Founders Online, National Archive) https://founders.archives.gov/?q=Dufour&s=1111311111&r=7 Includes French transcription, English translation, editorial notes.
8 Nov 1804	"Comptes des Avoirs de la Famille Dufour en Amerique, Rendu au Père"	ISL, Indianapolis	SSSC, pp. 224-233	Dufour family accounts & arrangements, made prior to Jean Jaques Dufour's return to Switzerland. SSSC provides both a transcription (in French) and its English translation.
20 Feb 1805	Letter to Thomas Jefferson, by John Brown	LC, Washington, D.C.	IW, p. 41	Brown was a Kentucky senator. His letter accompanied two casks of First Vineyard wine, transported to Jefferson by Jean François Dufour. May be viewed online at https://founders.archives.gov/?q=Dufour&s=1111311111&r=5

23 Feb 1805	Letter to John Brown, by Thomas Jefferson	UV, Charlottesville	IW, p. 42 (photo)	Jefferson critiques the wine. Can be viewed online at https://founders.archives.gov/?q=Dufour&s=1111311111&r=9
25 Jul 1805	"Letter from a Father in Switzerland for his Children in America," by Jean Jaques Dufour, Sr.		PMM, vol. 13, no. 8, pp. 348-352	Available online (Google Books). This is a sermon authored by Jean Jaques Dufour, Sr. addressed to his children in America.
15 Jan 1806	Document delegating power of attorney to Jean François Dufour by Jean Jaques Dufour			Jessamine County Deed Book B, County Deed Books, Jessamine County, Kentucky, p. 163.
Feb 1806	Advertisement for prospective investors			Jean Jaques Dufour sought investors for his yet-to-be patented steam engine through ads published in the *National Intelligencer and Advertiser*, (Washington, D.C.) on February 19, 21, and 24, 1806.
22 Feb 1806	Letter to James Madison, by John Brown	LC, Washington, D.C.	IW, p. 45	James Madison Papers. This letter and a First Vineyard wine sample was transmitted to Secretary of State James Madison by Jean Jaques Dufour. https://rotunda.upress.virginia.edu/founders/default.xqy?keys=FOEA-print-02-01-02-1433
23 Mar 1806	"Journal of the Pennsylvania Wine Company"	APSL, Philadelphia		Cited on p. 45 in IW. Jean Jaques Dufour attended a meeting of the Pennsylvania Wine Co. and inspected their vineyard.
6 Jun 1806	Custom house "Certificate for John James Dufour of Switzerland and then Kentucky in America"	Plymouth & West Devon Record Office, U.K.		Locator/Reference = 1/674/2/9 Plymouth Municipal Records / Municipal Papers / Alien Papers and Passports. Due to the war, Dufour paid an unintended visit to England. See IW, p. 46.

Date	Title	Source	Reference	Notes
9 Oct 1811	"New Swisserland," by John Francis Dufour			Published on November 2, 1811 in *The Weekly Register*, Vol. 1, pp.139-140. May be viewed online at https://earlyushistory.net/niles-register/
6 Jan 1812	"Passeporte, Canton de Vaud en Suisse"	CW, Dallas Texas		Aimé Dufour's passport, issued by the Canton de Vaud.
22 Dec 1812	"Petition to Congress by John James Dufour and Associates"		TP, Vol. VIII, pp. 224-225.	A petition wherein the Swiss colonists request an extension to their scheduled repayment.
10 Jun 1813	Letter to Samuel McKee, by Jonathan Jennings		TP, Vol. VIII, p. 260	Jennings, then a territorial delegate to Congress, vouches for the Swiss colonists.
24 Jul 1813	"Forward", by Daniel Debeltaz		IW, p. 57	Promoting the wines of New Switzerland then available in Cincinnati. Published on July 24, 1813 in *The Weekly Register*, Vol. 4, p. 344. May be viewed online at https://earlyushistory.net/niles-register/
2 Aug 1813	"An Act Giving Further Time to the Purchasers of Public Land, Northwest of the River Ohio, to Complete Their Payments"		USSL, Vol. 6, p. 126	
Oct 1813	"Vevay," by John Francis Dufour		IW, p. 56	Published on October 5, 1813 in the *Kentucky Gazette*, p. 4, column 4. May be viewed online at http://nyx.uky.edu/dips/xt7tqj77tn2z/data/0947.pdf

Date	Title	Location	Reference	Notes
31 Oct 1814	"Petition to Congress by Vinedressers of Switzerland County"		TP, Vol. VIII, pp. 311-312	
11 Sep 1815	"Comparution and acte de non Conciliation"	ISL, Indianapolis		A judgment concerning the disputed will of Abram Michel Reymond, a Swiss émigré to America, for whom Jean Jaques Dufour had served as executor.
13 Jun 1817	Land patent – for land sold to John James Dufour and associates	ISL, Indianapolis		"completion of payments recorded on reverse"
13 Jan 1825	Circular soliciting information about vine culture	IHS, Indianapolis	IW, p. 86 (photo)	In the broadside collection of the IHS. The circular was distributed by J. Francis Dufour, apparently to gain data for inclusion in The Vine-Dresser's Guide. (see IW, p. 87.)
Re. 19 May 1825	Description of the Dufours meeting Lafayette			*Lafayette in America*, by A. Lavasseur, translated by John D. Godman. Corey and Lea, Philadelphia, 1829. Vol. 2, pp. 175-177. May be viewed online through Google Books.
Dec 1825	"Cultivation of the Vine, by an American Navy Officer," by William Wilkins			Published in *American Farmer*, December 9, 1825, vol. 7, pp. 300-301. May be viewed online at https://earlyushistory.net/american-farmer/ Describes Dufour's efforts at First Vineyard.
1826	"The American Vine-Dresser's Guide" by John James Dufour		AVG (1826)	Probably about 500 copies were printed, and perhaps half that amount sold, since 205 copies were included in the estate of J. J. Dufour upon his death in 1827. Today copies are scarce.

Missing Documents

One can reasonably assume that a considerable amount of correspondence, journals, account books, etc. authored by the Dufours (on both sides of the Atlantic) is now lost. The following list merely records a few items whose former existence has, in one way or another, been documented.

Letter from Jean Jaques Dufour to "mons parens," mailed from Philadelphia on July 14, 1798. (See SSSC, p. 285.)

Letter from Jean Jaques Dufour to "mons parens," mailed from New York City on July 19, 1798. (See SSSC, p. 285.)

Letter from Jean Jaques Dufour to ? Daniel Dufour, mailed from New York City on July 23, 1798 (See 1800 Lettre.)

Jean Jaques Dufour's First Vineyard Journal. (See IW, p. 20.)

October 15, 1779 letter from Jean Jaques Dufour to Daniel Dufour. (See 1800 Lettre.)

Daniel Dufour's March 14, 1800 letter to Jean Jaques Dufour. (See 1800 Lettre.)

Original edition of the April 30, 1800 Compact, bearing the signatures of Daniel Dufour, David Golay, Philippe Berney, Joseph Meylan, and Jean Pierre Daniel Borralley.

The last page or pages of Daniel Dufour's letter to Jean Jaques Dufour, dated 26 June 1800. It apparently described the impact of Napoleon's march through Vaud in June 1800. (See 1800 Lettre.)

1800 passport for Daniel Dufour, giving his physical description. (See TDS, p. 39.)

Daniel Dufour's journal, from which the account of the colonists' voyage to America was originally obtained. (See TDS, pp. 20-25.)

Jean Jaques Dufour's travel journal describing his return to America in 1816, if not more. (See IW, p. 63.)

Documents (copies) concerning the Swiss Dufours given to Bettie Dufour Smith by the Swiss Consul. (See TDS, p. 50.)

www.ingramcontent.com/pod-product-compliance
Lightning Source LLC
Chambersburg PA
CBHW041538220426
43663CB00002B/68